Harvey Rosen

Melon Garnishing

Harvey Rosen

Robert J. Rosen, *Editor*

Kevin M. O'Malley
Artistic Coordinator

**With full-color photos
and step-by-step instructions**

Recognition

Dedication:

To A Great Loving Family...
Ann, Vicky, Debbie, Larry, Bob, Jon

Special Thanks To:

Keffier V. Adkins
Art Director/Artist

Vince Serbin
Photographs

Stephen H. Smith
Turlock Fruit Co.

Deborah Alison Stapel
United Fresh Fruit & Vegetable Assoc.

National Watermelon Assoc.

Florida Watermelon Assoc.

Texas Watermelon Assoc.

Published by:
International Culinary Consultants
P.O. Box 2202 Elberon Station
Elberon, New Jersey 07740

ISBN 0-9612572-3-7

Printed in U.S.A.

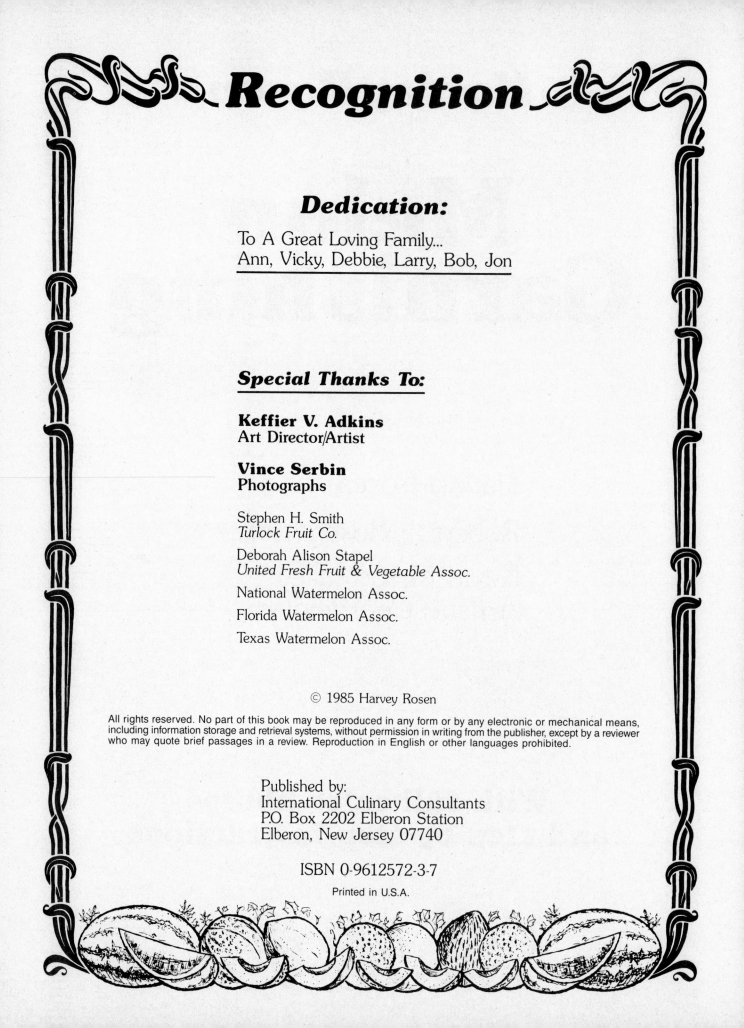

~From The Author~

Before undertaking to write a "How To" book on melon garnishing I thought long and hard; a book dedicated solely to creating artistic centerpieces from melons has never been attempted. I have written this book for a wide ranging audience, from the garde manger chef, like myself, to the weekend gourmet. Each will be able to follow my simple technique and create beautiful garnishes to add a special touch to any occasion.

During the development of this book I received invaluable artistic assistance from Chef Kevin O'Malley, GM to whom I am most grateful. Kevin has been actively involved as a garde manger chef and instructor for many years and is currently an instructor of garde manger at Hudson County Community College.

I invite you to study and enjoy the following illustrations, stencils and easy step by step instructions to perfect a unique and beautiful art.

Chef Harvey Rosen GM

Table of Contents

Melon Garnishes

History

Generally there are two melon families: The Muskmelons, which are native to Asia and the watermelons, native to Africa. The watermelon is appropriately named since it is 92% water. The Muskmelons were named because of the aroma of the fruit. "Musk" is from the Persian, meaning a kind of perfume; and "melon" from the Latin "Melopepo" meaning "apple-shaped melon."

Although melons are thought of as fruits, they are actually berries and are treated like vegetables in the garden. Therefore, properly speaking, melons are vegetables. Melons are usually planted in clumps on mounds or hills of soil. They grow on vines that creep along the ground for 6 to 10 feet or more.

Watermelons and muskmelons are of the Cucurbitacae family. Other cucurbits include pumpkins, squashes, gourds, and cucumbers. It is a most interesting plant family because it develops a tremendous vegetative growth and large melons from an apparently insignificant and inadequate root system. The plants are trailing annuals with stems as long as 15 feet and branched tendrils. Melons bear for one season only and must be replanted annually in temperate areas. The melon ripens from mid to late summer or early autumn, depending on the variety. In northern temperate areas melons are not an easy crop. They are susceptible to many diseases.

Melons need delicate handling; they must be protected from contact with damp ground, and they need large quantities of space and nutrients to grow well. Melons can be grown successfully in regions where minimum night temperatures average no less than 55 degrees F and minimum daytime temperatures are no lower than 80 degrees F throughout the growing season.

Melon seeds are edible. Dry them, put them in a fry pan, and pour some salted water over them. Stir over the heat until the water has evaporated. They make an excellent snack.

History

Melon can be frozen to last all year long. Cut firm melon into balls or cubes and place them in freezer containers. Then, for each pint, mix ½ cup sugar with 1½ cups water and heat until the sugar dissolves. Chill this mixture, then pour over the melon pieces and freeze.

A cool well-vented place is best for storing all types of melons. If the melon is not quite ripe, it may be ripened in a warmer area.

Melons are excellent food nutritionally. They are low in sodium and provide a good source of vitamins A and C, potassium, and other minerals.

They also provide fiber to the diet. Melons are a nearly perfect food for dieters, 100 grams of melon has only about 30 calories.

They are low in calories and exceedingly rich in vitamins and minerals.

WATERMELONS

The culture of watermelons goes back to prehistoric times. In the 1850's, David Livingston, the famed missionary explorer, established that Africa was the place of the watermelon's origin. He found great tracts of watermelon growing wild in the Kalahari Desert and the semi-tropical regions of Africa. There is some evidence that indicates possible American origins as well. For example, early French explorers found Indians growing watermelons in the Mississippi Valley.

Odd names for watermelon in Arabic, Berber, Sanskrit, Spanish, and Sardinian are all unrelated, indicating a great antiquity of culture in lands around the Mediterranean and east as far as India.

History

Watermelon cultivation goes back at least 4,000 years to the Egyptians whose artistic remains have recorded them. There is no name for the watermelon in the ancient Greek and Latin languages, and it was probably not known to these cultures much before the Christian era. It was probably introduced into southern Europe by the Moors early in the Christian era. The watermelon reached China where it was called "si-kua" or melon-from-the-east, about the tenth century A.D. and reached East Russia before then. The watermelon was introduced to Britain in 1597. The early colonists took watermelons to America and they are now grown in about half of the states, but mainly in California, Florida, Texas, Georgia, and South Carolina.

By the sixteenth century the watermelon was cultivated in Europe wherever it could be grown satisfactorily, and was described extensively by 16th and 17th century European botanists. The watermelon was distributed throughout the remainder of the world by African slaves and European colonists. It was carried to Brazil and the West Indies, to the islands of the Pacific, to New Zealand and Australia. Watermelons are now cultivated on all continents throughout the warm regions of the globe.

The watermelon consists of a firm outer rind, a layer of white inner rind flesh ½ to 1 inch thick and an interior, colored, edible flesh in which the seeds are imbedded. Watermelons are round to oblong with smooth, hairless skin. They weigh, depending on the variety, from 10 to 50 pounds, although watermelons as large as 140 pounds have been grown. The skin color ranges from light green to almost black and can be solid, striped, or marbled. The flesh may be cream-color, yellow, pale red, red, or scarlet.

In other parts of the world, watermelon is eaten in different ways. In southern Russia, beer is made from watermelon juice. The juice is also boiled down to a heavy syrup like molasses for its sugar. In Iraq and Egypt and elsewhere in Africa, the flesh of the watermelon is used as a staple food and animal feed as well as a source of water in some dry districts. Particularly in Asia, the seeds are roasted, with or without salting, and eaten as a snack.

History

High quality in watermelon is largely dependent upon high total sugar content. Other factors determining high quality are deep red color and pleasant texture of the edible flesh. Maturity is often difficult to determine without plugging, cutting out a small section, and testing. Usually ripe watermelons of good quality are firm, symmetrical, fresh looking with an attractive waxy bloom, and with good characteristic color for the variety. As a watermelon ripens, the white underbelly, where it contacted the soil, develops a creamy-yellow hue. If a melon is very hard and is white or very pale green on the underside, it is probably immature. If so, don't undertake to ripen it. In the watermelon, total sugar content does not increase after it comes off the vine. Watermelons should have good red flesh, be crisp and not mealy or water soaked from bruising.

If you are a watermelon ''thumper'' from way back, forget it! Thumping will get you nowhere.

Color is the best key to ripeness in watermelons. A yellowish underside, regardless of the rich green color of the rest of the melon, is a good sign of ripeness. A watermelon is somewhat like a book, in that you can't always tell its contents by its cover. When you go to buy a whole melon, look for one that is symmetrically shaped and has a velvety bloom - a dull, rather than a shiny surface. The underside should be turning from white or pale green to a light yellowish color.

Avoid ''white heart'' in watermelons -- a hard white streak running lengthwise through the melon . Seeds, too give a clue to ripeness. If the melon is fully matured, the seeds are usually dark brown or black. (Only one variety, the Improved Garrisonian, has white seeds.)

Most retailers charge slightly more for cut watermelons. It is well worth it! In this way, you can see the maturity of the melon -- the only sure way of selecting a good watermelon.

At home, watermelons should be kept refrigerated until served. They are available from March through October with their season peaking June through August.

History

There are a number of varieties of watermelon: small round melons weighing 4 to 6 pounds, large oblong types weighing 20 to 40 pounds and seedless watermelons weighing 10 to 20 pounds. The Sugar Baby and the slightly heavier, sweeter, yellow-fleshed Yellow Baby from China are excellent small "icebox-sized" watermelons. Of the large watermelons the greenish gray skinned Charleston Grey; the round, light and dark green striped Crimson Sweet; oblong striped Klondike; round, dark green Black Diamond (Cannonball or Florida Giant); and light and dark green striped, oblong Jubilee are the most popular. There are also a few Chinese varieties of watermelon -- the warty skinned Bitter Melon and the white haired fuzzy Melon.

Seedless watermelons are not ready available, but two good varieties include the Burpee Hybrid Seedless and Triple sweet seedless. Much attention has been focused on breeding seedless watermelons. These are not a major market variety.

The normal watermelon (diploid number) has 22 chromosomes. Triploids (3n or 33 chromosomes) and tetraploids (4n or 44 chromosomes) have been developed in an effort to produce seedless watermelons. Japanese scientists, especially, have been actively researching watermelon breeding since 1939. Diploids, triploids, and tetraploids can be recognized by distinctive rind patterns characterisitc of their chromosomal number.

Seedless watermelons are produced by crossing a tetraploid melon with a diploid melon. The hybrid resulting from this cross is triploid, which is characteristically sterile. When a triploid is fertilized with pollen from regular seeded melons (diploid) the resulting fruits are seedless.

MUSK

There are three classes of Muskmelons: the nutmeg or netted melons (variety reticulatus), rather small melons with net ribbed rind; the cantaloupe or rock melons (variety cantalupensis) with a hard frequently furrowed, warty or rough rind; wintermelon (variety indodorus), large, nearly odorless melons, with flesh varying from white to yellow or light green, maturing late and keeping in winter.

History

This group includes the Casaba, Crenshaw, Persian, Honey Dew and related melons. The winter melons are generally listed with the cantaloupes because their cultural needs are similar. But they are in a separate subspecies, inordorus, meaning they lack fragrance.

Plant breeders have created numerous hybrids between all three muskmelon groups. This helps explain why seed catalog houses for the sake of simplicity group them all together.

The nutmeg or netted Muskmelons are recognized by their distinctive, raised netting which may be coarse like crochet work or like fine lace. This is why they are also called "embroidered" melons in France and "netted" melons in Britain and America. They may be sharply segmented or grooved, with green or yellow-orange skin, and the flesh ranges from green to salmon-pink.

Muskmelons constitute a commercial crop usually outranking in value all other vegetables marketed fresh, except tomatoes and lettuce. Americans know their most famous melon of this type as the cantaloupe, which is a misnomer. The true cantaloupe is not grown commercially in the United States.

The Muskmelon is native to the Near East areas including Persia, Turkey, and Middle Asia. It is certain that Muskmelons were cultivated in very ancient times. Examinations of records from the first century A.D., found in Alexandria and now in the Louvre, seem to show melons represented with other fruits in a cornucopia on a vase-painting. They are also depicted on bas-reliefs and etchings, proving that they were undoubtedly grown in the Nile Valley at the time of the Pharaohs. It seems, however, that Muskmelons were not cultivated in Europe until the Middle Ages, except perhaps in southern Spain which was occupied by the Moors. Introduced from the Orient via Armenia, the Muskmelon appeared in the fifteenth century, brought by Charles VIII to France from Naples in 1495.

History

Since the Renaissance, an improved cultivation and relations with the East have introduced better varieties into our gardens. The first record of Muskmelons grown in the New World was made by Columbus in 1494 upon return from his second voyage. The presence of Muskmelons is reported among Indians near Montreal in 1535, and Virginia in 1609. It is also reported that Indians grew Muskmelons in the vicinity of Philadelphia prior to 1748.

Fortunately, nature has provided an excellent means for gauging the ripening process of most cultivars of muskmelons. As the melon approaches maturity, a light abscession crack develops at the joint where the melon is attached to the stem. When this crack completely encircles the joint, the melon is at the "full slip" stage and contains the maximum amount of sugar. Some varieties can be harvested at the "full slip" stage for local markets, but must be harvested earlier if they are to be transported to distant markets.

Unfortunately, certain muskmelons, including the Honey Ball, Honey Dew, Persian, and Casaba, abscess only after the melons are overripe. Means other than abscession must accordingly be used to gauge harvest maturity in these Muskmelons. Color of the ground spot and slight changes in skin color, usually yellowing of part or all of the skin, are measures of maturity in these Muskmelons. In addition, the blossom end becomes slightly soft and yields to gentle pressure at maturity. Considerable experience is required to harvest these cultivars successfully.

CANTALOUPES

The true cantaloupe is not the melon grown in the United States. The true European cantaloupe is Cucumis melo variety cantaloupensis. They are medium sized Rockmelons with a rough, warty, or scaly surface, without netting. The melons grown in the United States are Cucumis melo variety reticulatus which includes all the netted melons (they are reticulate) and includes what we call cantaloupes and also Persians and other netted Muskmelons.

History

The word cantaloupe comes from the Italian "cantaluppi" and literally means "song of the wolf." It is the name of a castle and former summer residence of the Popes near Rome. This is where the original cantaloupe introduced from Armenia was cultivated.

Sweetness, fine texture, flavor, and juiciness are quality factors of cantaloupes. The melon must be mature at harvest since the sugar content does not increase after picking, although it can soften and change the types of sugars. If a cantaloupe has been picked at right maturity so it will ripen properly, it will be well netted or webbed and have a smoothly rounded, depressed scar with no jagged ends at the stem end. This is the "full slip" condition because the stem has come off fully and smoothly when the melon was given a slight lift by the picker. If the stem end is rough with portions of the stem adhering, the cantaloupe was not fully mature when picked and will not be as satisfactory as the "full slip" melon.

Consumers far from growing areas rarely find ready-to-eat melons at the store. If cantaloupes are shipped a long distance, as most are, they must be picked while firm. If this is done at "full slip," they need only to soften. This process may take three or four days.

Cantaloupes should be of adequate size, 5 or more inches in diameter, not small or runty or misshapen. They should not be mottled, have growth cracks, be shriveled, flabby or badly bruised. If they show any degree of decay, mold, or soft sunken spots, they should be rejected.

Look for cantaloupes with a well defined netting on the skin and a musk-like sweet aroma. The background color of the skin of a ripe cantaloupe should be slightly yellow, not green and the blossom end will yield slightly to finger pressure. The flesh should be thick, sweet, salmon to orange in color, and moderately soft.

Cantaloupes should not be eaten too soon. Give them time to take on a yellow background appearance, acquire an aroma and soften. This can be done by allowing them to ripen at room temperature in the home.

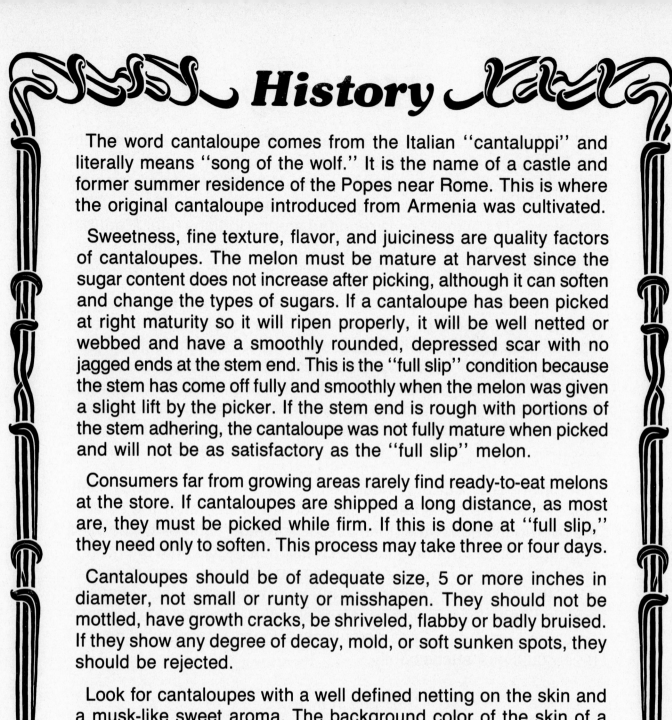

History

Cantaloupes are a good source of vitamin A and C. Half a cantaloupe 4 inches in diameter provides more than the RDA of vitamin A and 100 percent of the RDA of vitamin C. Cantaloupes are low in calories. The edible part of half a melon 5 inches in diameter, 185 grams, provides only 60 calories. Cantaloupes also provide good quantities of calcium, phosphorous, iron, potassium, and magnesium.

Cantaloupes are available year round with homegrowns peaking during June through August. Some excellent varieties are Burpee's Hybrid, Delicious 51, Mainerock Hybrid, Hearts of Gold, SJ45, Topmark, Magnum 45, and Harvest Queen.

HONEY DEWS

The Honey Dew is of the species melo which includes all muskmelons and belongs to the variety inodorus which includes so-called "winter" melons such as Casabas, Honey Balls, Crenshaws, and Persians. The Honey Dew was introduced to the United States about 1900.

The Honey Dew melon is quite large, slightly oval, 6 to 8 inches in diameter, weighing 5 to 7 pounds. The surface is smooth with an occasional streak of cork-like net. The skin color is ivory, white, or greenish white turning creamy white with pale yellow streaks or blotches at harvest maturity. The flesh is moderately thick, green, firm, and very sweet.

The ripening of the Honey Dew is associated with definite external color changes, an increase in sugar, a decrease in starch and acidity, and the release of characteristic aromatic emanations. To be of the most desirable eating quality, Honey Dew melons should be fully ripe, with creamy outer color and waxy feel to the surface, and have sweet light green flesh that is juicy and fine textured. Honey Dews remain attached to the stem at maturity and are cut from the vine when harvested. Therefore, the condition of the stem does not indicate the stage of maturity.

Severe bruises, cuts or other damaging defects can be readily detected if present. "Sugar Cracks" and small wart-like proliferations or ridges of tissue do not detract from the eating quality. Do not buy over ripe melons; they have a bitter flavor. Decay generally appears as sunken, water-soaked spots on which pink, black, or near black fungal growths may be present. In advanced stages, such sunken spots may penetrate the rind and seriously affect the flesh. The decay mentioned is not due to market decay in the usual sense. but to chilling injury.

Keep Honey Dews at room temperature to fully ripen them before serving. If they are ripe, refrigerate or serve immediately.

Honey Dew melons are available throughout the year but their peak season is June through October. Quality is at a low point from December through February. Two excellent varieties are the Honey Mist and Honey Drip.

CASABA

The Casaba is a globe-shaped melon with a pointed stem end and averages between 4 and 7 pounds. The skin has deep, lengthwise furrows and turns golden yellow at maturity. The Casaba is a sweet melon with white flesh without aroma. To select Casabas look for melons that are golden yellow with a slight softening at the blossom end. Sniffing them will be of no help since the Casaba has no aroma. It is available from July through November with its season peaking in September and October. Two excellent varieties include the Sungold Casaba and the Golden Beauty Casaba.

CRENSHAW OR CRANSHAW

The Crenshaw melon has a golden rind tinged with green when ripe. It can be smooth or slightly ribbed. The Crenshaw can be round or oblong with a pointed stem end, weighing 7 to 9 pounds. The flesh is salmon-pink colored, spicy and moderately sweet. Crenshaws are available from July through October, but peak season is August. A ripe Crenshaw has a fragrant melon aroma and a tender blossom end that will yield slightly to finger pressure. An excellent variety is Burpee's Early Hybrid Crenshaw.

History

HONEYBALL

The Honeyball melons are much like the Honey Dews but are smaller and rounder with meshed brown netting. When they are ripe, they are soft and sweet with a slight fragrant aroma. The flesh is light white-green color and juicy. Honeyballs are available from June through November.

PERSIAN

Persian melons are round with dark green rind covered with a pale yellowish netting. The flesh of the Persian is orange-pink with a fine texture and a mildly spiced flavor. These melons are the most difficult to choose. Select Persians with a smooth stem end, slightly soft blossom end and fragrant aroma. As the melons ripens, the rind turns a lighter green. Persians are marketed from July through October and their size ranges from 6 to 9 inches in diameter, weighing 3 to 8 pounds.

JUAN CANARY

This melon was first planted in the United States in 1972. The Juan Canary is a bright yellow and oblong in shape. The flesh is sweet and white with a pinkish tinge around the seed cavity.

SANTA CLAUS OR CHRISTMAS MELON

The Santa Claus muskmelon resembles a small oval watermelon with a mottled yellow and green rind. Its flesh is pale green in color, sweet, and mild. The melon is so named because of its long shelf life and ability to be stored for consumption at Christmas.

SPANISH

The Spanish melon is similar in taste to a Crenshaw, spicy, and moderately sweet. It has a dark green corrugated rind. A ripe Spanish melon has a tender blossom end and a pleasant aroma. The peak season is July through October.

History

OGEN

The Ogen is named after the Israeli Kibbutz Ha-Ogen which started its commercial development. It is now grown throughout the world. The ogen has a green skin with orange lines, dividing it into sections. The flesh is green and sweet tasting of Anjou pears. They are small melons 5½ to 6 inches round so one melon should be allowed for each person. It is selectively available from spring to mid-winter.

GALIA

The Galia melon has a bark-like or netted appearance which turns from green to golden yellow when ripe and sweet. It has green flesh and is a bit larger than its relative, the Ogen. It is named after the daughter of the man who raised it.

LAVAN

This is a round Honey Dew with a bit more flavor.

VEDRANTAIS AND CHARENTAIS

These are two varieties of the true European cantaloupe. They have green, warty skin and fragrant, sugary, orange flesh. In many places this melon is available all year long. It keeps well when stored in a cool, dry place and ripens after several days in a warm room.

SHARLYN

The Sharlyn is a netted, oblong shaped melon with orange flesh. When the melon is ripe the exterior has a golden-tan appearance.

ORANGE FLESH

This melon is a cross between a Honey Dew and Cantaloupe. The exterior of the Orange Flesh melon should be creamy white like a Honey Dew. The interior is bright orange with a sweet Cantaloupe flavor.

Tools

These helpful tools were designed to save time while giving melon garnishes a professional flair.

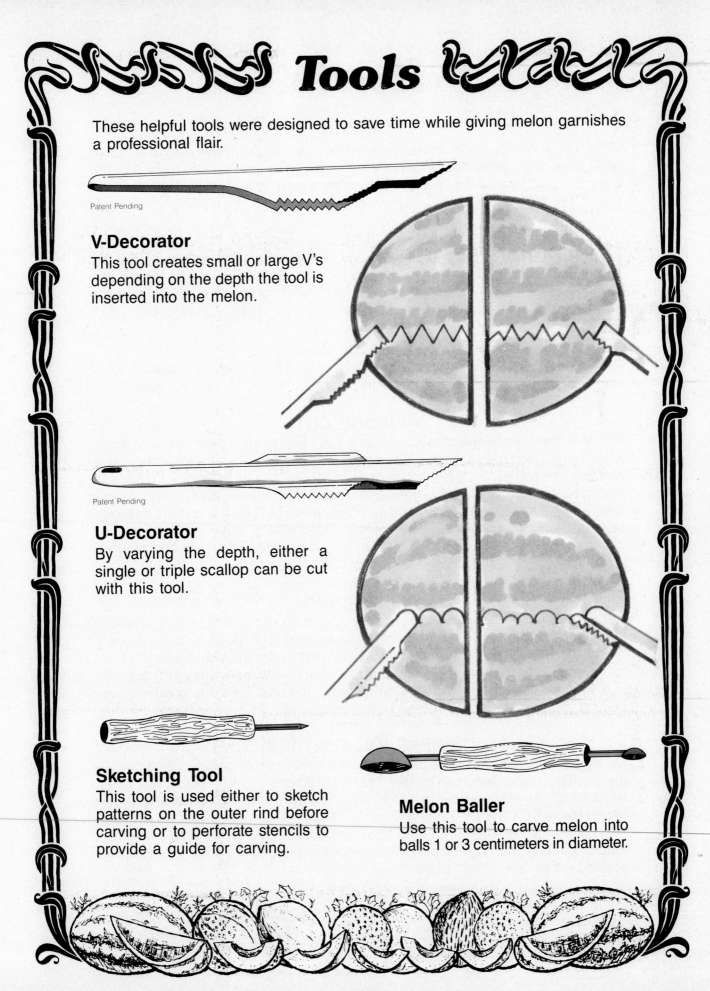

Patent Pending

V-Decorator

This tool creates small or large V's depending on the depth the tool is inserted into the melon.

Patent Pending

U-Decorator

By varying the depth, either a single or triple scallop can be cut with this tool.

Sketching Tool

This tool is used either to sketch patterns on the outer rind before carving or to perforate stencils to provide a guide for carving.

Melon Baller

Use this tool to carve melon into balls 1 or 3 centimeters in diameter.

Hints

DESIGN

Most melon centerpieces focus on an object carved from the rind of a melon with some flesh remaining. Outline the design on the melon and cut along the lines removing the excess melon. Round the necessary areas of flesh and then apply the detail work.

BASES

Bases are used to provide stability, height and dimension to melon sculptures. They should not be too large or overshadow the principal object. Bases can be carved into boulders, waves or other solid objects to fit the specific theme of the display. An example is to place the seahorses on a base of waves.

MELONS FOR CARVING

Firm melons should be chosen for the carvings. Ripe melons which should be used for the melon balls and fruit salad are more difficult to carve.

V-WEDGE CUT

The V-wedge cut is the most important cut used to decorate melon centerpieces. It is used to put finishing touches on shells, wings, tails and other body parts of the sculpture. It is important to practice the cut on excess pieces of melon before actually carving the centerpiece to avoid mistakes. A sharp knife held at a 25 degree angle is used to make this cut. Make a cut on one side and then the other to meet at the center. Remove the V-wedge section. The cut can be made from a point and then fanned out (clam shell) or can be used alone (wings). (See step-by-step instructions Page 41.)

PRESERVING

Unflavored powdered gelatin or aspic jelly can be used to coat and preserve the melon sculptures. The jelly can be brushed, ladled or sprayed on. To prepare clear unflavored gelatin sprinkle into cold water and allow to bloom (soften) for five minutes. Then heat over a double boiler to approximately 100 degrees F. until clear. Do not over heat. Cool slightly and use. Be sure to remove the excess moisture from the melon before applying.

CONTAINERS VS. CENTERPIECES

Certain melon sculptures are used as containers while others serve as centerpieces. The centerpiece can be used as the highlight of a buffet or dinner party. Sliced fruit, salad or whole fruit can be placed around the centerpiece. The centerpiece sets the theme of the party (Example: Lovebirds for an anniversary). The melon sculptures that have containers can be used to serve fruit salads directly from the display. Small containers can be used as individual appetizers or light lunch entrees.

Hints

SUPPORT MATERIAL

Wooden skewers and round (not flat) toothpicks are used extensively to hold the sections of melon sculptures together. Keep the toothpicks dry to preserve their rigidity. To provide stability to large melon sections larger skewers or ¼ inch wooden dowels can be used.

PATIENCE AND PRACTICE

Some of the melon sculptures require patience and practice. Follow the guides, diagrams and instructions set forth and with time you too can make the most detailed melon sculptures. You don't have to be an artist to make these sculptures, you only need a desire to try.

BACKGROUND

The arrangement can be highlighted with small twigs, mint leaves, lemon leaves, ferns, baby's breath, dried flowers or other accessories.

ARRANGEMENT

Balance is an important concept to keep in mind when putting a melon sculpture together. Objects can be placed at different heights to vary arrangement. Symmetry is also important. Occasionally back away a few feet to check the overall balance of the arrangement.

SERVING SUGGESTIONS

Honeydew tastes great when served with lime, lemon, thinly sliced salami, crumbled bacon or blue cheese.

Watermelon can be combined with chopped celery and pecans, then folded into whipped cream or softened cream cheese.

Melon can be cut into shapes and topped with cottage cheese, vanilla ice cream or sherbet or frozen yogurt.

Melons should be chilled and can be served with ginger.

Use your blender or food processor to make watermelon juice and freeze it to make naturally sweet watermelon popsicles.

Sugar is often served for the sweet tooth because even the sweetest melon will be enhanced by a fine dusting of sugar.

Cut a plug in a melon and fill with port wine, chill, then slice and serve in wine sauce or liquor.

Melon can also be served with prosciutto ham or chicken.

Recipes

Melon is not only a tasty food by itself, but makes a delicious ingredient to dessert, snack and salad recipes. The following is a collection of the finest melon recipes available. If you have a favorite recipe that uses melon, please share it with us.

FRENCH WATERMELON TORTE

Shell:
3 tablespoons butter
1½ cups whole almonds, ground
4 1-oz. squares semi-sweet chocolate
⅛ teaspoon salt
2 tablespoons sugar
Filling:
1 8-oz. package cream cheese, softened
1 cup cream-style cottage cheese
1 teaspoon vanilla
½ cup sugar
1¼ oz. envelope unflavored gelatin
2 tablespoons water
½ cup heavy cream, whipped
Topping:
2 cups watermelon chunks, seeded
¼ cup sugar
3 to 4 tablespoons cornstarch
   (depends on juice of melon)
Chopped almonds

To make shell: In small skillet, melt butter. Add ground almonds and cook, stirring until lightly roasted. Add chocolate, stirring until melted. Stir in salt and 2 tablespoons sugar. Press mixture into bottom and 1½ inches up the sides of an 8-inch springform pan. Chill.
To make filling: In a large bowl, beat together cream cheese, cottage cheese, vanilla and ½ cup sugar until fluffy and smooth. In a small saucepan, combine gelatin and water. Cook over low heat, stirring until gelatin is dissolved. Stir into cheese mixture, mixing thoroughly. Fold in whipped cream. Spoon into chilled crust and let cool.
To make topping: Place watermelon chunks, sugar and cornstarch into blender and puree. Place pureed watermelon mixture into saucepan and heat, stirring until thickened. Remove from heat and let cool. Spoon cooled mixture over torte, leaving a small border around edge. Press chopped almonds into border. Chill.

WATERMELON-IN-A-POCKET

3 cups watermelon balls
2 cups cooked, diced turkey or chicken
½ cup celery, chopped
1 bunch scallions, finely chopped (green tops, too)
1 small green pepper, chopped
½ cup chopped pecans
Dressing:
4 or 5 pita "pocket" breads, halved
leaf lettuce

Prepare dressing: Combine all first six ingredients, mixing gently but thoroughly. Line pocket bread with lettuce. Spoon in watermelon/turkey filling and enjoy.
Dressing: Stir together ½ cup plain yogurt; ¼ cup mayonnaise; 1 tablespoon lemon juice; 1 tablespoon chopped, fresh parsley; 1 clove garlic, minced; 1 teaspoon Italian seasoning; 1 teaspoon salt and ½ teaspoon pepper. Cover and chill ½ hour for flavors to "mellow".
This salad may also be served on a plate, over a bed of lettuce. Makes 8 to 10 half sandwich/salads.

WATERMELON MINI-POPS

3½ cups watermelon, cubed and seeded
½ cup sugar
½ cup water
2 teaspoons fresh lemon or lime juice

Place watermelon in a food processor or blender and puree. Measure 3 cups puree. In a small saucepan mix sugar and water together and simmer 3 minutes. Remove from heat; stir in watermelon puree and lemon or lime juice. Turn into ice trays or plastic popsicle molds. Freeze until very mushy, then insert a popsicle stick if using ice cube trays. Freeze until firm. Makes about 30 popsicles.

Recipes

WATERMELON SHRIMP SALAD IN A CREAM PUFF BOWL

Salad:
2 cups watermelon balls or cubes
2 cups frozen, cooked, small shrimp, thawed
½ cup diced celery
½ cup shredded Swiss cheese
½ cup raisins — optional
½ cup dairy sour cream
¼ cup mayonnaise
curly lettuce leaves
slivered almonds for garnish — optional, or fresh mint sprig

Cream Puff Bowl:
½ cup water
¼ cup butter
½ cup flour
⅛ teaspoon salt
½ teaspoon sesame seeds
¼ teaspoon celery seeds — optional
2 eggs

Combine the watermelon balls, shrimp, celery, Swiss cheese and raisins. Toss lightly and chill. Just before serving toss lightly and stir in sour cream and mayonnaise. Spread curly lettuce along the inside of the cream puff bowl and pile watermelon shrimp salad on top. Garnish with slivered almonds or a fresh mint sprig. Cut in wedges to serve. Servings: 4 or more.

Note: You may use chicken or ham in place of the shrimp. You may freeze the cream puff bowl until ready to use up to 1 week. When ready to use, remove and let thaw about 1 hour.

Cream Puff Bowl: Heat oven to 400°F (Mod. hot). Heat water and butter to boil in a saucepan. Stir in flour, salt, seeds, at once. Stir vigorously over low heat until mixture leaves side of pan and forms a ball, about 1 minute. Remove from heat. Cool slightly, about 10 minutes. Add eggs, one at a time, beating until smooth and velvety. After each addition spread batter evenly in bottom of a greased glass 9-inch pie pan (have batter touching sides of pan, but do not spread up sides.) Bake 45 to 50 minutes. Cool slowly away from drafts. The puff forms a bowl (high on sides and flat in center). Fill with Watermelon Shrimp Salad.

SUMMERTIME CHICKEN SALAD

2 cups cooked, cubed chicken
1 cup persian melon cubes, peeled and seeded
½ cup diced celery
⅓ cup cashew nuts
¼ cup sliced scallions
creamy yogurt dressing
iceberg lettuce leaves

In a medium bowl, combine chicken, melon cubes, celery, cashew, scallions and creamy yogurt dressing. Mix well. Cover and chill one hour. Serve on a bed of iceberg lettuce. Serves 4.

HONEYDEW WALNUT SALAD

If you have an underripe honeydew this is the recipe to use. The firm texture of the honeydew is what makes this salad extra special.

4 cups slightly under-ripe honeydew, cubed
1 cup roasted walnuts
4 tablespoons minced parsley
1 cup diced celery
1 cup diced sweet red pepper
4 tablespoons lime juice
2 teaspoons honey
2 tablespoons white vinegar
½ cup vegetable oil
1 teaspoon salt
dash pepper

In a large salad bowl, toss together the honeydew, walnuts, parsley, celery, and red pepper. Mix together the remaining ingredients and pour over the salad. Toss to coat. Serve at once or chill and serve. Yield: 6 servings.

WATERMELON SALAD WITH CELERY-NUT DRESSING

4-ounce cream cheese, softened
2 tablespoons mayonnaise
⅓ cup heavy cream, whipped
1⅓ cups celery, thinly diced
3 cups watermelon balls, chilled bright green lettuce leaves
½ cup pecans, chopped

Beat cream cheese with mayonnaise until smooth and fluffy. Fold into whipped cream; add celery. Arrange watermelon on salad greens and top with celery-cheese dressing. Sprinkle with chopped pecans. Serves 6.

Recipes

AUNT ELAINE'S PICKLED WATERMELON

4 quarts watermelon rind	1 tablespoon whole cloves
4 quarts cold water	3 cinnamon sticks
1 cup salt	1 lemon, thinly sliced and seeds removed
2 cups vinegar	
7 cups sugar	

Pare watermelon rind by removing the outer green and inner pink portions. Cut rind into 1 inch squares. Cover with saltwater solution. Let stand 6 hours or overnight. Drain; rinse well. Cover with fresh cold water in large saucepot. Cook until tender, about 10 minutes. Do not overcook. Drain. Tie spices in cheesecloth bag. Combine vinegar, sugar, 4 cups water and spices to saucepot; boil 5 minutes. Remove spice bag, retaining cinnamon sticks. Pour syrup over watermelon rind and add lemon slices. Let stand overnight. Heat watermelon rind and lemon slices in syrup to boiling; cook until rind is translucent (about 10 minutes). Pack hot rind into clean hot jars. Add 1 piece cinnamon stick from the spice bag to each jar. Cover with boiling syrup, leaving ½ inch headspace; seal. Process pints in boiling water bath 10 minutes. Yield: 4 to 6 pints.

WATERMELON MOUSSE

2½ cups watermelon, cubed and seeded	1 tablespoon lemon or lime juice
1 envelope unflavored gelatin	1 cup heavy cream lemon or lime slices and melon balls for garnish
1 cup sugar	

Puree watermelon in food processor, electric blender or by mashing through a coarse sieve. Measure 2¼ cups puree. Heat remaining 2 cups pureed watermelon in a medium saucepan over low heat until almost boiling. Add softened gelatin and stir until dissolved. Remove from heat; add the sugar and lemon or lime juice. Chill, stirring occasionally, until the mixture mounds slightly when dropped from a spoon. In a separate bowl, whip the cream and fold it into the watermelon mixture. Turn the mixture into a 1 quart mold. Freeze. Unmold and garnish with lemon or lime slices and melon balls. Serves 6.

WATERMELON PRESERVES

1 lb. watermelon rind cubes	2 cups sugar
2 quarts water	1 quart water
2 tablespoons lime (calcium oxide)	½ lemon

Trim off outer green skin and pink flesh, using only greenish-white parts of rind. Cut rind into 1-inch cubes, and weigh. Soak cubes for 3½ hours in limewater (2 quarts water and 2 tablespoons lime). Drain and place cubes in clear water 1 hour. Again, drain off water and boil 1½ hours in fresh water, then drain. Make a syrup of 2 cups of sugar and 1 quart water. Add rind and boil 1 hour. As syrup thickens, add ½ lemon, thinly sliced, for each pound of fruit. When the syrup begins to thicken and the melon is clear, the preserves are ready. Pack preserves into hot sterilized jars, add enough syrup to cover, and seal.

WATERMELON MUFFINS

1 cup sugar	1 teaspoon cinnamon
1 teaspoon soda	1 cup pecans, chopped
1 cup water	½ cup margarine
½ teaspoon cloves	2 cups all purpose flour
¼ teaspoon salt	1 teaspoon vanilla
1 cup (10-oz. jar) watermelon pickles, chopped	

Combine the sugar, water, chopped watermelon pickles, margarine and spices in a saucepan and bring to a boil. Cool at least 30 minutes. Sift the flour, soda and salt together and add to cooled mixture. Fold in the nuts and vanilla. Fill muffin cups, lined with paper cups, about half full. Bake at 350 degrees for about 25 minutes. Cool and frost with the following.

Frosting

¼ cup margarine	¼ teaspoon cinnamon
1 teaspoon vanilla	2 cups sifted confectioners sugar
2-3 tablespoons cream	

Combine the margarine, cinnamon, vanilla and sugar. Add enough cream to make a nice spreading consistency.

Recipes

MELON-PINEAPPLE GLAZE

½ cup pineapple juice
1 cup melon juice
½ cup brown sugar
2 teaspoons prepared mustard
½ teaspoon ground cloves
1 tablespoon soy sauce

Mix all ingredients, use to glaze hams, pork, chicken, or meat kabobs. As a garnish try watermelon balls dipped in stiffly beaten egg white and rolled in cinnamon sugar.

WATERMELON FONDUE

1 cup undiluted evaporated milk
2 cups chocolate chips
Watermelon Balls
¼ cup butter
1 teaspoon vanilla extract

Melt over low heat in a double boiler. Place in fondue pot. Dip melon balls in the hot chocolate sauce. For a simpler recipe, melt 1 package chocolate chips; dip melon cubes or balls in hot sauce.

FESTIVE WATERMELON CAKE

1 box white cake mix
1 tablespoon plain flour
1 3-oz. pkg. mixed fruit jello
¾ cup Wesson oil
1 cup cut-up watermelon pieces
4 eggs

Sprinkle flour over cake mix. Add jello, oil and watermelon. Mix thoroughly with electric beater, adding eggs one at a time. Divide batter into 2 greased and floured 8-inch pans. Bake for about 30 minutes at 325 degrees. Ice when cool.

Topping

1 stick of margarine
1 box of powdered sugar
½-1 cup of cut-up watermelon

Soften margarine and add sugar. Blend in the watermelon gradually until a spreading consistency is reached. Red food coloring may be added. Spread the topping over the cake.

WATERMELON ICE CREAM PIE

24 graham cracker squares
¼ cup corn oil margarine
1 cup watermelon
1 quart vanilla ice cream, softened

Blend flour crackers on low speed 10-15 seconds or until fine crumbs form. Empty into medium bowl. Repeat process with remaining crackers. In small saucepan melt margarine. Remove from heat. Add to cracker crumbs; mix until crumbs form ball. Press mixture into 9″ pie plate. Refrigerate 1 hour. Place watermelon in blender container. Cover. Blend on low speed 30 seconds. Swirl mixture through ice cream. Firmly pack ice cream into crust. Cover. Freeze several hours or until firm. Makes one 9″ pie.

WATERMELON SPICE PIE

1½ cups watermelon rind
1 teaspoon cinnamon
¼ teaspoon cloves
2 teaspoons flour
½ cup raisins
1 2-crust pie pastry
1 cup sugar
⅓ teaspoon nutmeg
⅛ teaspoon salt
¼ cup vinegar
½ cup pecans, chopped

Cut green outer rind and most of pulp from watermelon rind; cut into ¼ inch cubes. Combine cubes with water to cover in saucepan; bring to boil, then simmer until tender. Drain. Add sugar, cinnamon, nutmeg, cloves, salt, flour, vinegar, raisins, and nuts to cubes; blend well. Pour into pastry shell; cover with pastry. Cut steam vents. Bake at 450 degrees until crust is browned. Reduce temperature to 350 degrees; bake until filling is set.

WATERMELON PIE

1 large box Mixed-fruit Jello
1 large size non-dairy whipped topping
¼ cup water
2 cups watermelon balls
Graham cracker crust

Fold together jello, water and non-dairy whipped topping. Fold in watermelon balls. Place mixture into graham cracker crust. Chill for 2 hours.

Recipes

WATERMELON PIZZA TORTE

Torte:
- 1½ cups white flour
- ½ teaspoon baking powder
- ½ teaspoon Cream of Tartar
- 2 eggs slightly beaten
- ½ cup sugar
- ½ cup butter or margarine
- 1½ cup evaporated milk

Watermelon Filling:
- ¼ to ½ of a small watermelon (about 4' cups of melon balls)
- 1½ cups Ginger Ale
- ¼ cup sugar
- 3 envelopes unflavored gelatin
- juice of one lime or lemon
- ½ pint whipping cream
- ¼ to ½ cup chopped nuts

Heat oven to 350°F. Grease 12 inch pizza pan. In large mixer bowl, combine all Torte ingredients, beat 3 minutes at medium speed. Spread batter into greased pizza pan. Bake about 25 minutes or until toothpick comes out clean. Cool completely in pan.

Dissolve gelatin in ½ cup ginger ale. Heat rest of ginger ale to boiling point. Add sugar and lime juice. Pour over gelatin and stir until dissolved. (Cool only slightly. Do not let it get too thick.) With small rounded spoon, make enough balls from watermelon. Arrange about 4 cups of watermelon balls on top of torte. Pour gelatin over melon balls. Refrigerate about 1 hour. When ready to serve, decorate with whipped cream around edge. Sprinkle top of torte only with nuts.

WATERMELON SHERBERT

- 1¼ cup water
- 1 tablespoon + 1 teaspoon lemon juice
- 2 cups watermelon juice
- ½ cup sugar
- ½ cup non-fat dry milk solids
- 2 egg whites, beaten stiff

Blend ½ cup water and sugar in heavy pan. Heat until sugar dissolves. Bring to a boil and simmer 5 minutes. Meanwhile place ¾ cup water and lemon juice in mixing bowl. Sprinkle non-fat dry milk solids over the surface and beat until mixture is thick and fluffy. Blend in watermelon juice and crushed watermelon; add syrup. Pour mixture into refrigerator tray and begin freezing. When partially frozen, remove from tray and beat with rotary beater. Fold in stiffly beaten egg whites. Return to freezer until frozen firmly. 12 servings.

WATERMELON-CINNAMON BUNDT CAKE WITH WINE SAUCE

- 1 cup butter, softened
- 4 eggs
- 1 tablespoon cinnamon
- 1 teaspoon salt
- 1 teaspoon lemon flavoring
- 2 cups diced watermelon (seeds removed)
- 2 cups light brown sugar, packed
- 3 cups whole wheat flour ("pastry" or "graham" *not bread flour*)
- 1 teaspoon baking soda
- 1 tablespoon red port

Grease the inside of a 3½ quart bundt pan very well, sprinkle with flour and shake out the excess. Preheat oven to 350 degrees.

Using the large bowl of an electric mixer, cream the butter and sugar together. Add the eggs and beat until fluffy. Sift the flour, cinnamon, salt, and baking soda together.

Slowly add the sifted ingredients to the sugar mixture. Add the watermelon, lemon flavoring, and port and mix until well blended.

Spread the batter evenly in the prepared bundt pan and bake at 350 degrees for 55-60 minutes — until top springs back when lightly touched.

Sauce:
- 1 cup red port
- 1½ teaspoon cinnamon
- 1 cup light brown sugar, packed
- 1 teaspoon lemon flavoring

2 cups watermelon juice (Mash or puree 4-5 cups diced, seeded watermelon. Strain, and then press the pulp against the strainer.)

Place the watermelon juice, port, sugar and cinnamon in a 2-quart saucepan over medium heat. Bring to a low boil. Stirring occasionally, boil steadily for 15-20 minutes — until the sauce becomes syrupy. Remove from heat and add the lemon flavoring.

Allow the finished cake to cool briefly in the pan. Then invert it onto a large plate. Slice when completely cool. Pour warm sauce over each serving.

Drinks

UNCLE JOHNNY'S MELON PUNCH

1 large watermelon

With melon standing on end, cut a thin slice off side so it will sit level. Remove top third of watermelon. Using a jar ring as a guide, trace scallops around top outside edge. With a sharp knife, carve scalloped edge, following tracing, scoop out fruit, leaving just a trace of red showing in bowl of melon. Chill the watermelon bowl.

Mix together the following to pour in the bowl:

1 6-oz. can frozen orange juice	4 cups watermelon juice (squeezed from the inside of the melon)
1 6-oz. can lemonade	
1 16-oz. can pineapple juice	4 cups sugar

Add enough water to make 2 gallons, chill; then fill the melon bowl. Add sprigs of mint. Decorate with an American Flag and Red, White and Blue streamers for a super centerpiece at parties or the 4th of July Picnic.

FRESH MELON JULEP

1 cup sugar	10 cups cantaloupe balls (about 3 cantaloupes)
¼ cup fresh mint leaves	
1 cup water	2 cups honeydew melon balls
2 tablespoons fresh lemon or lime juice	2 cups watermelon balls
¼ cup dark rum	fresh mint sprigs

Combine sugar and mint leaves with 1 cup water in a small saucepan. Stir over low heat until sugar dissolves, simmer 5 minutes. Remove from heat and pour through a strainer; discard mint. Stir in lemon or lime juice and rum. Cool. Combine cantaloupe, honeydew and watermelon with cooled mint-rum syrup. Chill several hours or overnight. To serve, spoon fruit into dessert dishes and garnish with sprigs of mint. Serves 8.

MELON DRIVER

1 oz. melon liqueur	½ lime
1 oz. orange juice	

Combine with ice and stir. Garnish with a slice of lime.

WATERMELON LEMONADE

2 cups fresh ripe watermelon puree*	½ cup sugar
½ cup fresh lemon juice	½ teaspoon grated lemon rind
	2 cups water

Combine watermelon, lemon juice, sugar and lemon rind in pitcher. Stir well to dissolve sugar. Mix in water. Chill. Serve in tall glasses over ice cubes. Makes about 1 quart. *To puree watermelon, remove rind and seeds. Press through sieve, food mill or food processor.

MELON COLADA

2 oz. melon liqueur	6 oz. pina colada mix
1 oz. rum	

Mix in blender, pour in chilled glasses and serve.

MELON COLLINS

1 oz. melon liqueur	1 oz. sweet and sour mix
1 oz. vodka	

Pour in glass, fill with soda and ice, stir and serve.

TROPICAL MELON

1 oz. melon liqueur	2 oz. half & half
½ oz. white rum	

Pour over ice, stir and serve.

MELON CREME

1 oz. creme de menthe	1 oz. melon liqueur

Pour over crushed ice in cocktail glass. Stir and serve.

MELON MARGARITA

1½ oz. tequila	1 oz. sweet and sour mix
½ oz. melon liqueur	

Blend and pour into salted glass.

Stencils

The following pages contain ½ size outlines for stencils of melon sculptures. Enlarge these to make full size stencils by transposing the figures from the book's ½ inch grid to a 1 inch grid. Hold the stencil against the melon rind and outline the figure with a sharp pointed sketching tool.

Then carve along the lines drawn. A sharp pointed sketching tool can also be used with full size vinyl stencils. Hold the stencil against the rind and puncture the vinyl and rind along the lines. Then carve the figure along the holes you have just punched. Additional full size vinyl stencils are available from International Culinary Consultants.

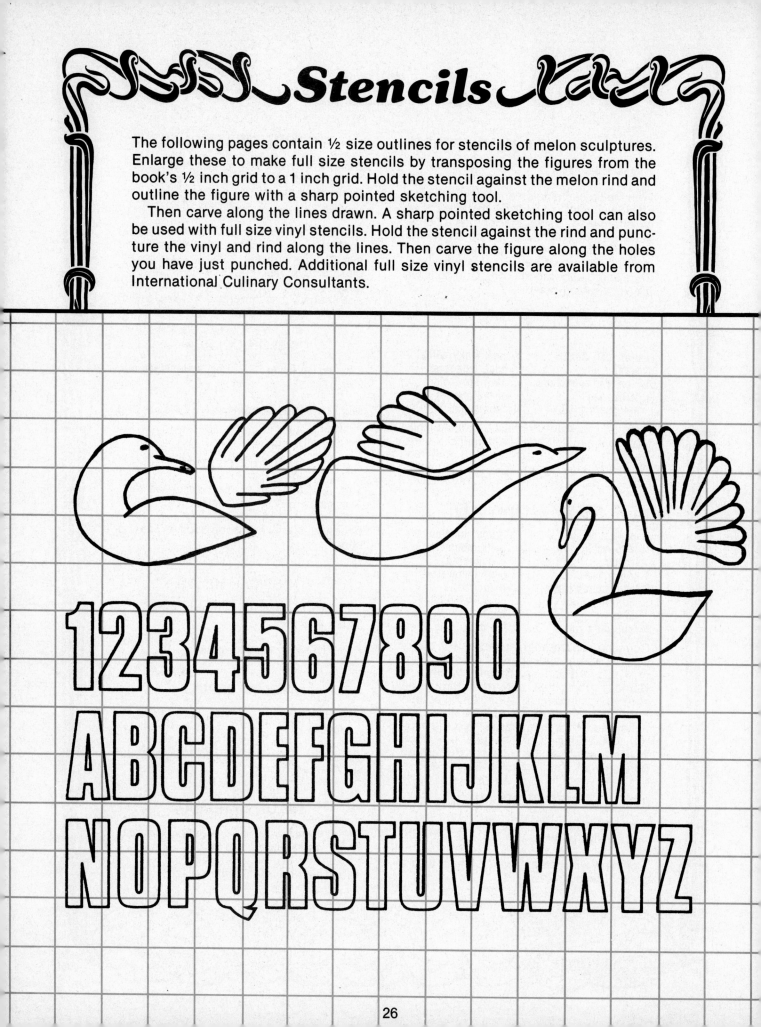

Galleon

Select an oblong watermelon for this centerpiece.

Cut a thin slice from the bottom of the melon to provide a stable base.

Use a knife or decorating tool to cut horizontally along the side of the melon.

Make the cut on a slight angle, making the bow (front) of the ship higher than the stern (back).

Remove the top section of rind and use it to shape the large center sail.

Shape the remaining sails from the rind of another melon and attach them to the ship with long wooden skewers.

Carve a triangular portion from a section of rind and attach it to the bow (front) of the ship.

A flag and rudder may be carved from rind and attached to the ship.

Place rectangular pieces of melon along the edges of the ship.

Push grapes and melon balls onto long wooden skewers and attach them to the side of the ship as oars.

Decorate the ship with blueberries, strawberries, melon balls or cherries.

Cut a thin slice from the bottom of a large watermelon to create a stable base.

Draw the outline of the ship as shown.

Using a sharp knife or decorating tool cut along the lines of the pattern just drawn.

To aid in the removal of the rind make a deep cut across the top section and remove this section in two pieces.

The sail can be made from a section of rind or heavy construction paper.

Messages for any occasion can be written on the sail.

Attach the sail to the ship with a long wooden skewer.

Cruise Ship

Choose a large elongated watermelon for this attractive centerpiece.

Cut the watermelon in half length-wise.

Cut a slice from the bottom of one half of the melon to create a stable base for the cruise ship.

This half will be used for the hull of the ship.

Carve the hull of the ship with a sharp knife as shown in the photograph.

Hollow out the bow (front) and stern (back) of the ship leaving the flesh of the melon in the center area.

Carve port holes around the hull of the cruise ship as shown.

From the remaining half of the watermelon cut slices approximately ¾" thick.

Trim off the rind from these slices and cut the flesh into appropriate rectangles or squares to form the various decks.

Stack these pieces on top of each other in the center of the cruise ship.

The larger pieces on the bottom and the smaller pieces on top will form the decks.

Carve the smoke stacks from a remaining piece of watermelon and attach with toothpicks to keep them from falling over.

Fill the bow (front) and stern (back) of the cruise ship with assorted fresh fruit.

Garnish the cruise ship with lemon leaves or ferns.

Cut ¼ from the end of a small melon for the base.

Cut three pieces from a melon as diagramed.

Draw the outline of the shell on the flesh side of the melon using a stencil made from the diagram provided.

Cut away the unwanted areas. Slightly hollow out the center of the inside.

Decorate the shells with V-wedge cuts from the edges to the center.

Attach two shells together with toothpicks and mount on the base.

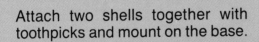

Fill with melon balls or other fruit.

Angel Fish

Carve the pieces for the angel fish from the rind of a melon using stencils made from the diagrams provided.
Carve and contour the flesh as shown.

Attach the fish to the base with wooden skewers and decorate the arrangement with lemon leaves or ferns.

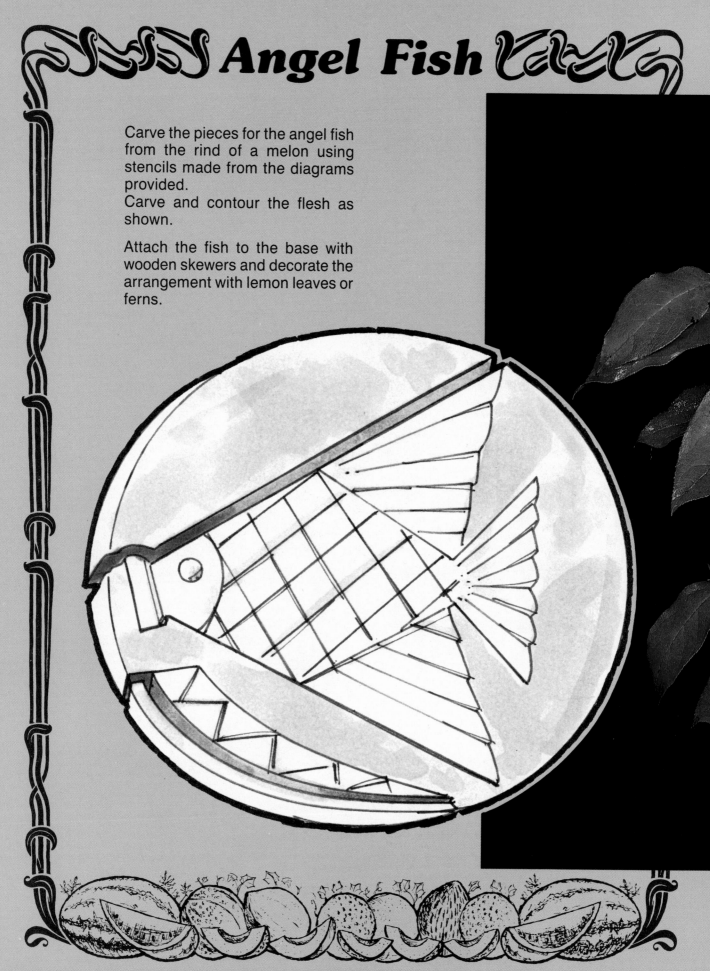

Sea Horse

Draw and then carve the waves of the base as shown.

Use stencils made from the drawings provided to carve the sea horses from the rind of a melon.

Contour the flesh and decorate with V-wedge cuts as shown.

Attach the sea horses to the base and decorate with ferns or lemon leaves.

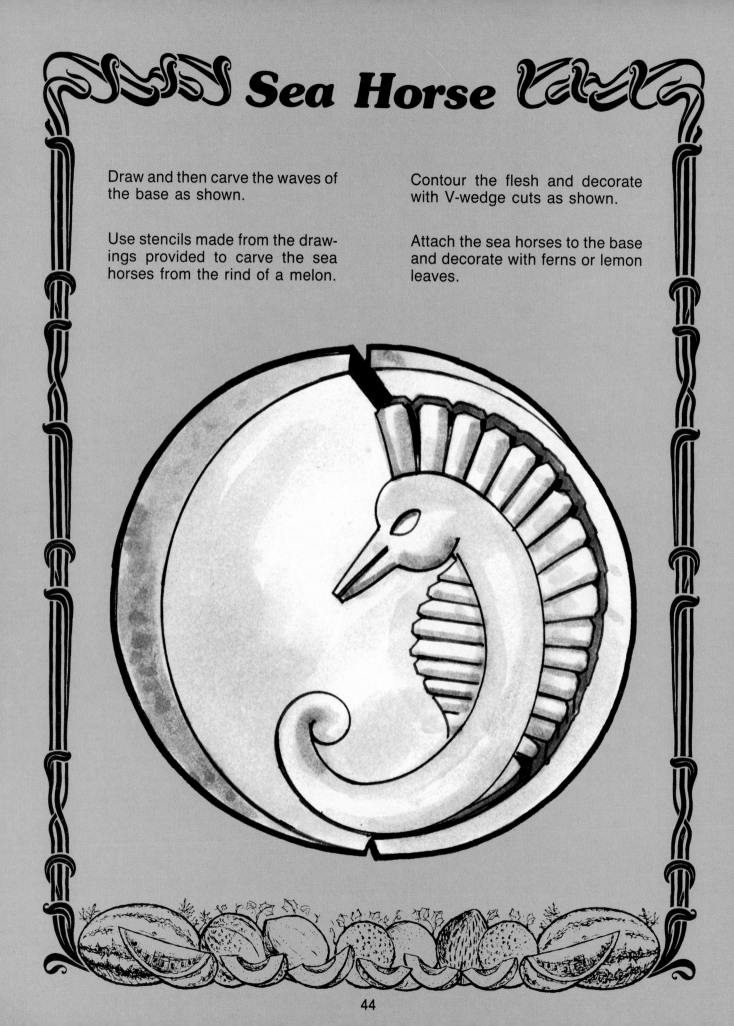

Dolphin

Carve the fins, bodies and tails of the dolphin using stencils made from the diagrams provided.

Contour and carve the flesh as shown.

Attach the fins and tails to the bodies with toothpicks.

Using long wooden skewers attach the dolphin to a base made from another melon.

Melon shells and ferns may be used to decorate the background.

Sword Fish

Cut a small slice from a large watermelon to provide a stable base.

Draw a straight horizontal line around the side of the melon.

Use a knife or decorating tool to form the decorated edge.

From the remaining rind carve the body and fins using stencils made from diagrams provided.

Cut away and contour the flesh as shown.

Attach the fins to the body of the fish with toothpicks and secure the fish to the base with long wooden skewers.

Decorate the background with lemon leaves or ferns.

Remove the flesh from the base and fill it with mixed fruit.

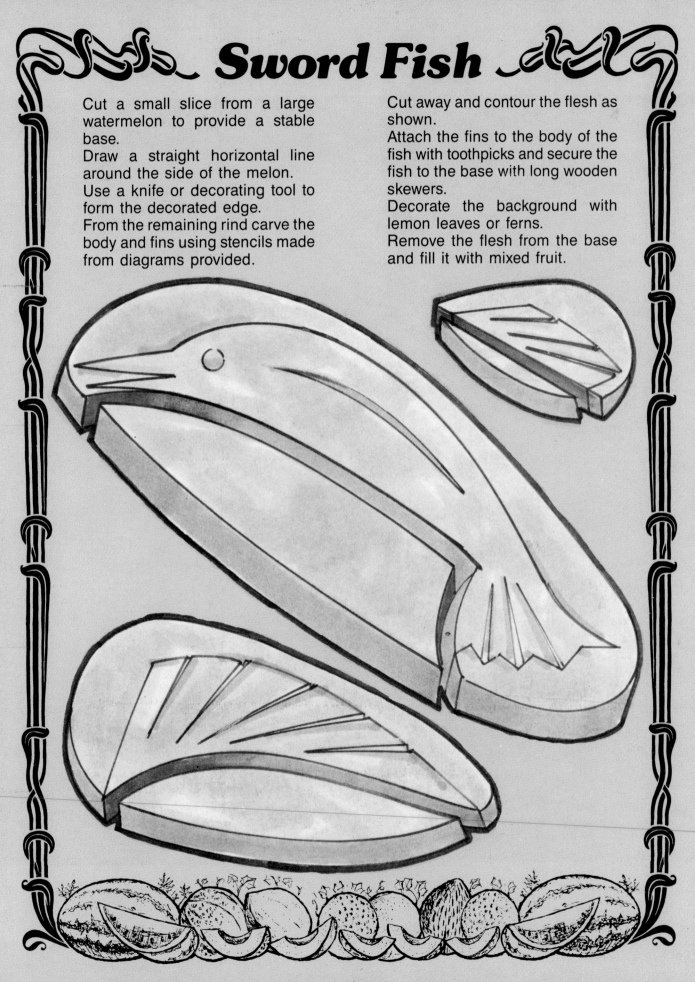

Whale

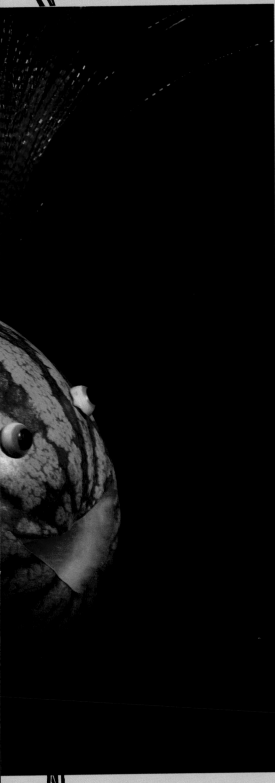

Choose a large oblong watermelon for this sculpture.

Cut a thin slice from the bottom to provide a stable base.

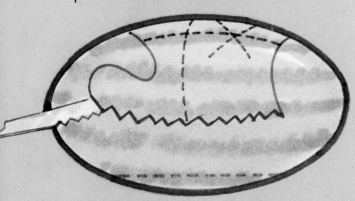

Draw the outlines for the whale as shown.

Use a knife or decorating tool to cut the decorated edge on the side and a knife to cut the tail and head.

Remove the top section of rind. It can be cut into pieces to aid in its removal.

Carve the mouth and eyes or plastic eyes may be obtained from a craft shop.

Hollow the shell and fill as desired.

Seal

From the rind of a melon, carve the shape of the seal's body and flipper using stencils made from the diagrams provided.

Carve away all of the flesh from the flipper, exposing the white rind. Contour the flesh of the body as pictured.

Use a seed for an eye and attach a melon ball to the seal's nose.

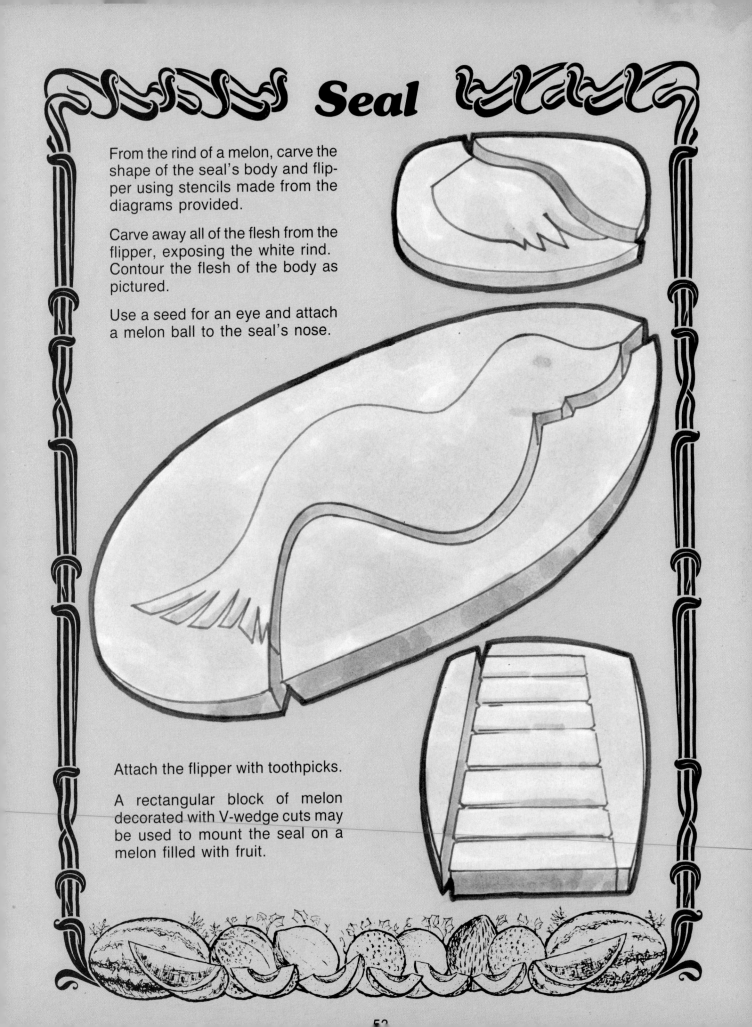

Attach the flipper with toothpicks.

A rectangular block of melon decorated with V-wedge cuts may be used to mount the seal on a melon filled with fruit.

Eagle

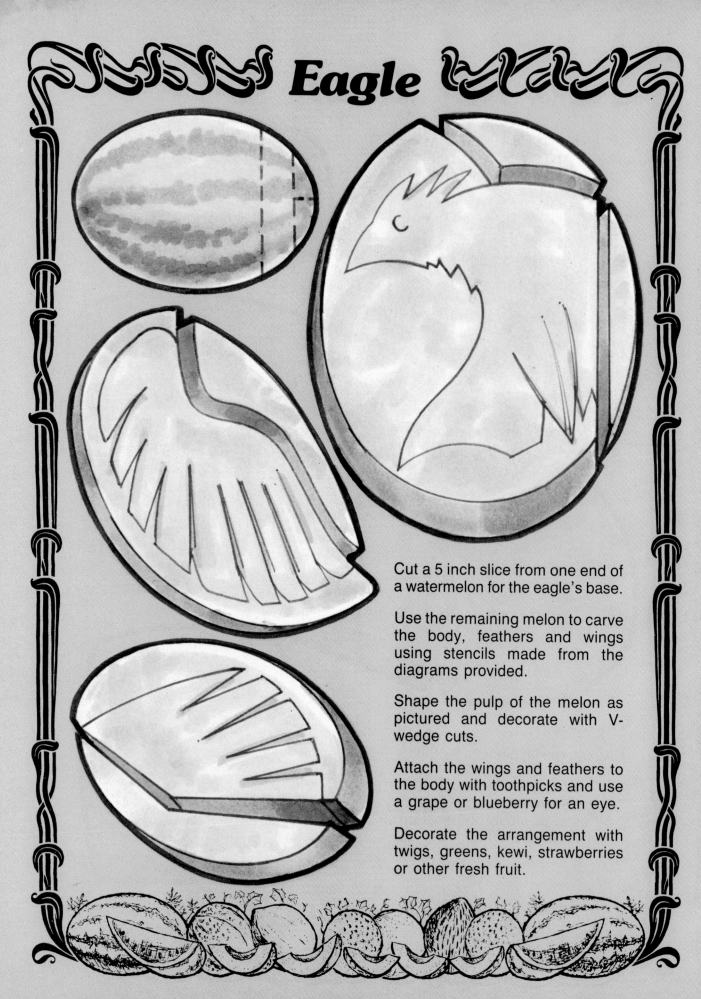

Cut a 5 inch slice from one end of a watermelon for the eagle's base.

Use the remaining melon to carve the body, feathers and wings using stencils made from the diagrams provided.

Shape the pulp of the melon as pictured and decorate with V-wedge cuts.

Attach the wings and feathers to the body with toothpicks and use a grape or blueberry for an eye.

Decorate the arrangement with twigs, greens, kewi, strawberries or other fresh fruit.

Swan

Draw and then carve the head and wings of the swan as shown. Use stencils made from the diagrams provided as a guide.

Use a sharp knife to cut along the lines but leave the beak attached to the body for stability.
Do not attempt to remove the top section in one piece.

From the remaining rind draw and then carve the tail and headpiece.

Attach the headpiece and tail with toothpicks.

Decorate the body and wings by carving grooves as shown.
Carve grooves for the mouth and eye and fill them with pieces of red licorice.

Trim the flesh and hollow the body.

Swan-2

Cut a slice from the bottom of a round melon to provide a stable base.

Draw the pattern for the swan as shown.

Use a sharp knife to cut along the lines drawn to form the swan.

Be careful to leave the beak attached to the feathers for stability.

Use a knife to hollow out an eye.

Do not attempt to remove the top section in one piece.

Cut it into quarters to aid in its removal.

Hollow the melon and trim the feathers so they are not too thick.

Use a melon ball scoop to form balls from the removed melon.

Fill the swan with melon balls, strawberries or desired fruit.

Turkey

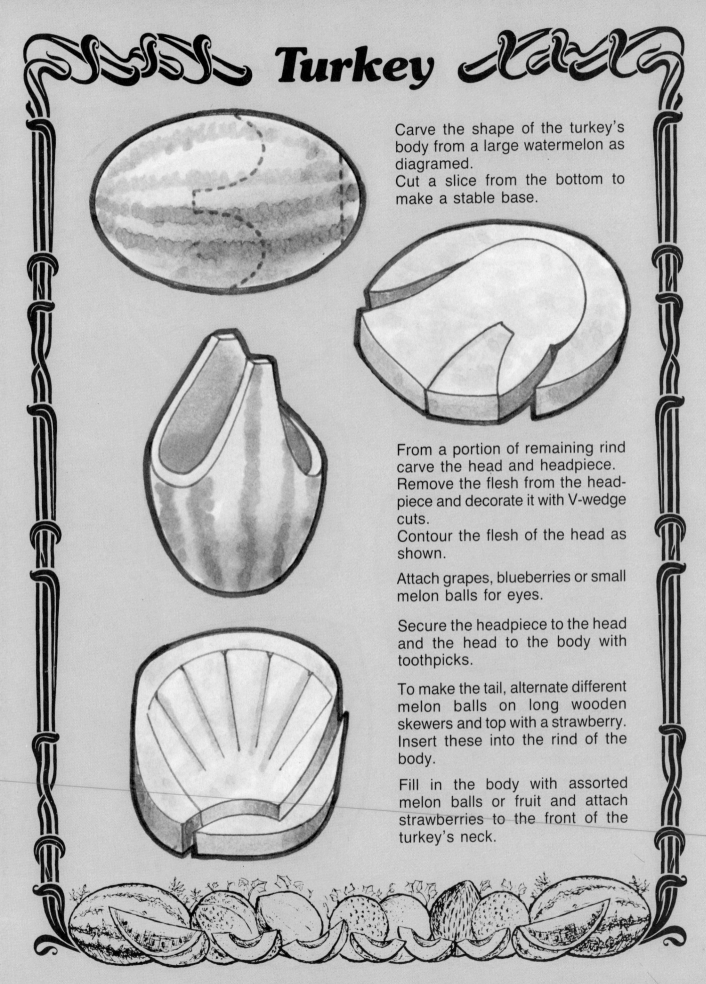

Carve the shape of the turkey's body from a large watermelon as diagramed.

Cut a slice from the bottom to make a stable base.

From a portion of remaining rind carve the head and headpiece. Remove the flesh from the headpiece and decorate it with V-wedge cuts.

Contour the flesh of the head as shown.

Attach grapes, blueberries or small melon balls for eyes.

Secure the headpiece to the head and the head to the body with toothpicks.

To make the tail, alternate different melon balls on long wooden skewers and top with a strawberry. Insert these into the rind of the body.

Fill in the body with assorted melon balls or fruit and attach strawberries to the front of the turkey's neck.

Peacock

Cut a thin slice from the bottom of a melon to provide a stable base. Draw and then carve the head and neck using a stencil made from the diagram provided.

The remaining rind is used to make the wings, headpiece and supporting tail section.

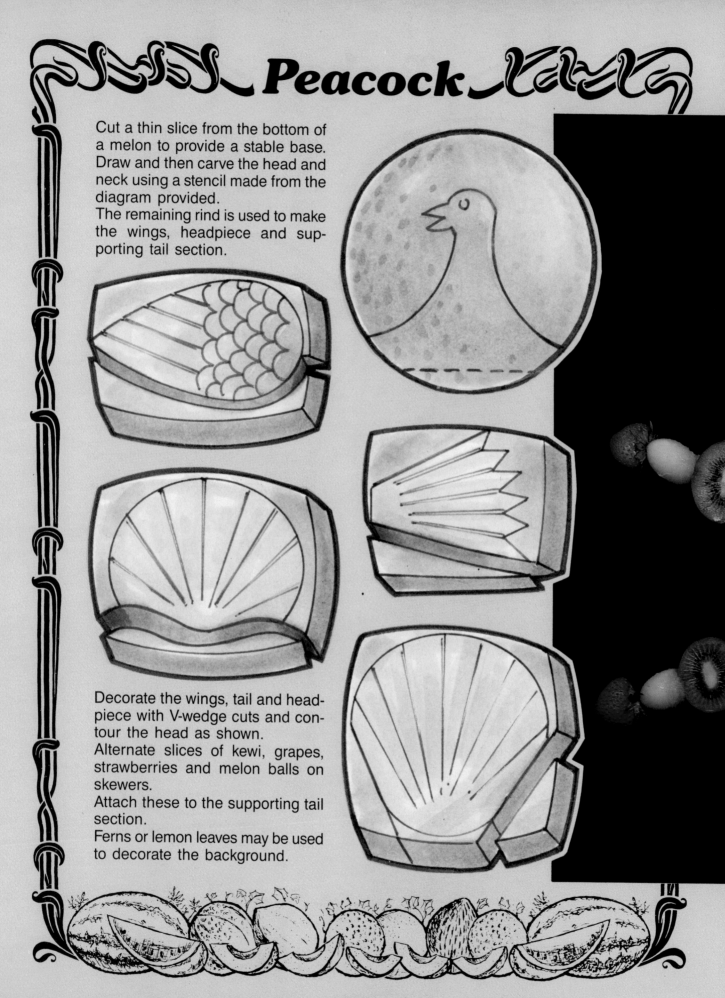

Decorate the wings, tail and headpiece with V-wedge cuts and contour the head as shown.

Alternate slices of kewi, grapes, strawberries and melon balls on skewers.

Attach these to the supporting tail section.

Ferns or lemon leaves may be used to decorate the background.

Dove

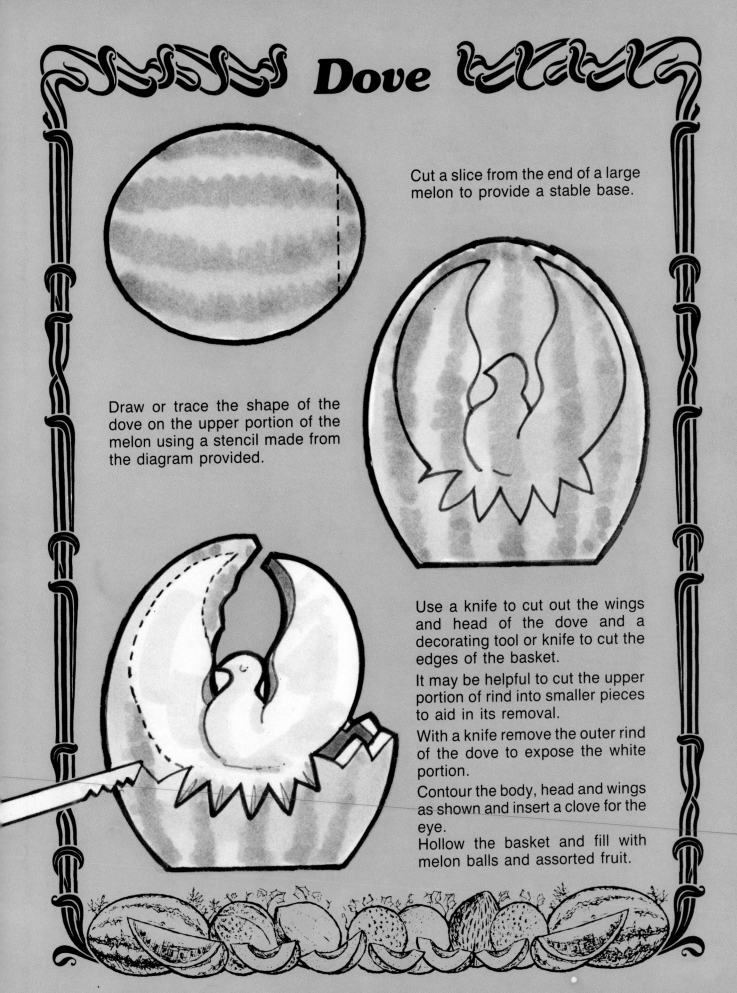

Cut a slice from the end of a large melon to provide a stable base.

Draw or trace the shape of the dove on the upper portion of the melon using a stencil made from the diagram provided.

Use a knife to cut out the wings and head of the dove and a decorating tool or knife to cut the edges of the basket.

It may be helpful to cut the upper portion of rind into smaller pieces to aid in its removal.

With a knife remove the outer rind of the dove to expose the white portion.

Contour the body, head and wings as shown and insert a clove for the eye.

Hollow the basket and fill with melon balls and assorted fruit.

Melon Cups

Lovely melon cups can be made from any melon variety.

Use a knife or decorating tool to cut the fancy edges.

Separate the two halves and hollow the centers.

These may be used separately.

Filled with melon balls or fruit they can be stacked and used as a centerpiece.

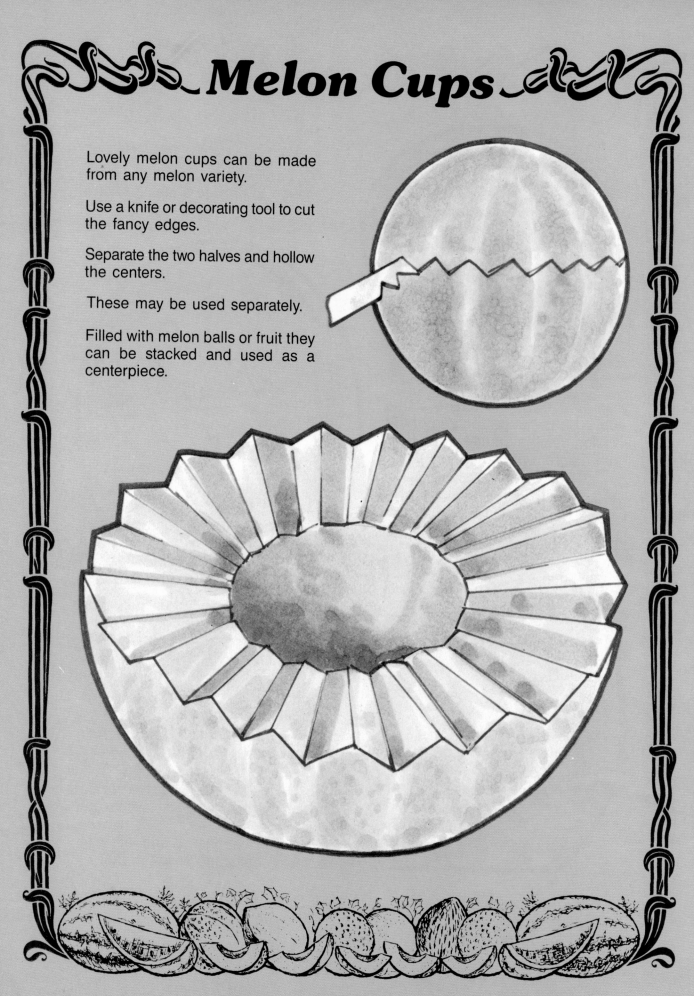

Donkey Head

Choose a large oblong watermelon for this centerpiece.
Cut a slice from the bottom of the watermelon to create a stable base for the donkey's head.
Carve two lines ¼ of the way from each end.
Remove the green and white portions of the rind from the center section, exposing the red flesh of the melon.
From the front and back sections remove just the outer green rind, exposing the white portion.

Cut a wedge from the front and scoop out some of the flesh for the mouth.
Carve the ridge around the mouth for lips and above the lips bore two holes for the nostrils.

Cut the ears and tongue from the rind of another watermelon.
Remove most of the flesh and the outer rind.
Attach these with toothpicks or wooden skewers.

Use the rind of a yellow canary melon (the watermelon could be used instead) to shape the teeth and attach them with toothpicks.

Create the headpiece from the top of a pineapple.
Trim the edges of the leaves and attach.

Make the eyes from a slice of kewi and lemon topped with a grape.
Cut sections from an apple and shape into eyebrows.
Garnish the donkey's head with sliced pineapple.

Baskets

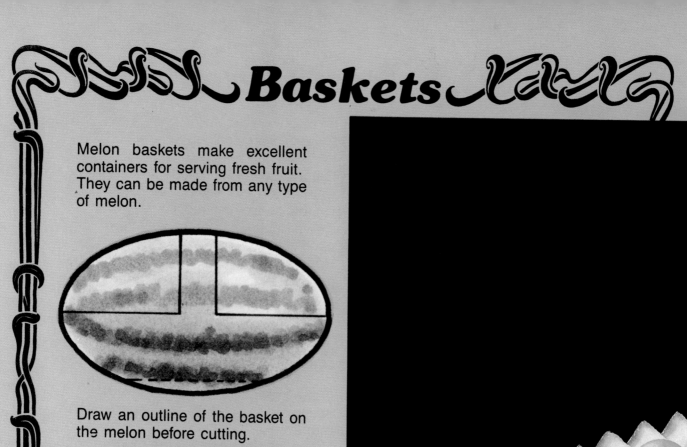

Melon baskets make excellent containers for serving fresh fruit. They can be made from any type of melon.

Draw an outline of the basket on the melon before cutting.

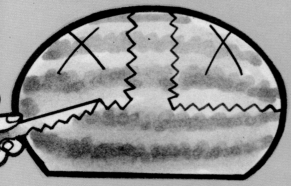

Use a knife or decorating tool to make a pattern along the edges. Be careful not to cut through the handle.

When cutting is complete, carefully remove the top quarter sections. Trim the flesh from the inside of the handle.

A melon baller can be used to shape balls to fill the basket. The outer rind of the basket can be decorated by carving out various designs.

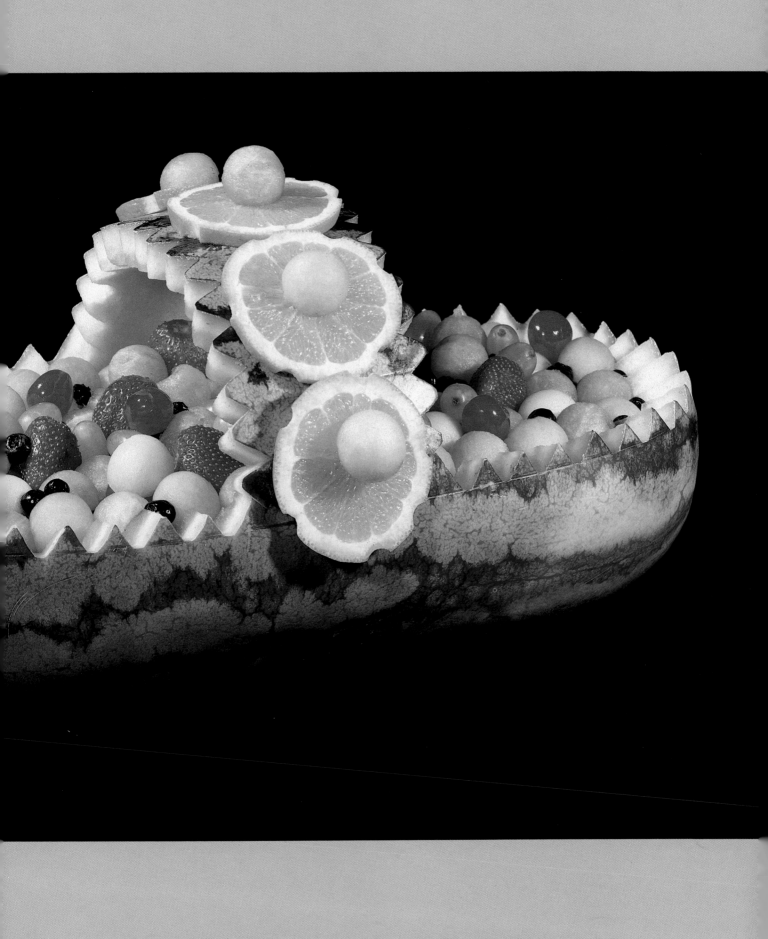

Baby Buggy

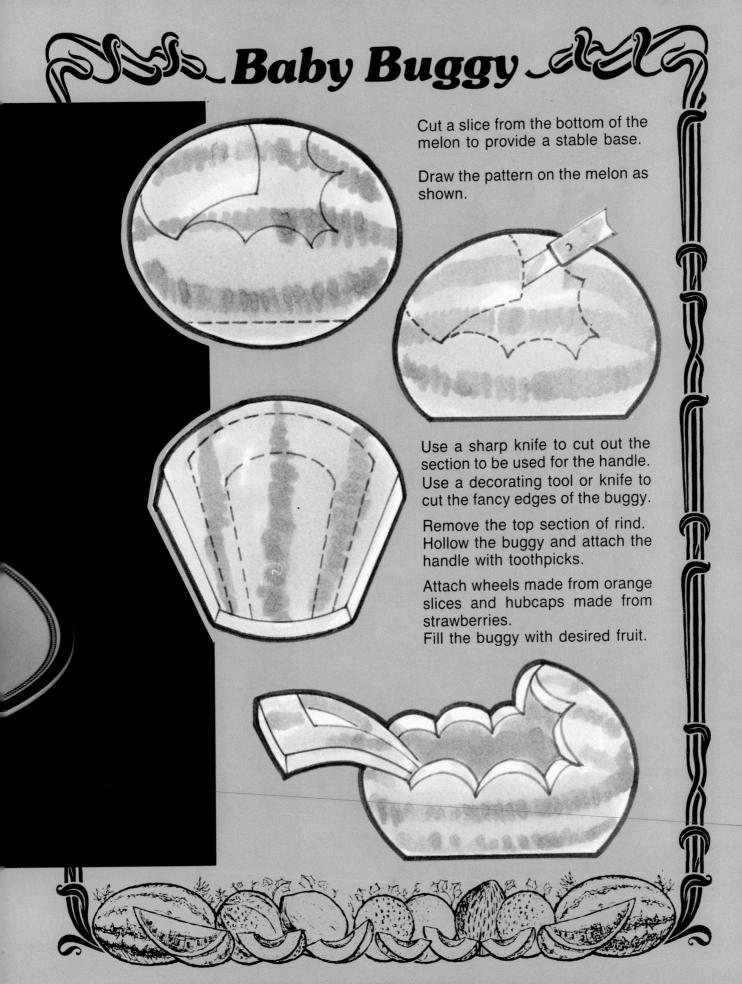

Cut a slice from the bottom of the melon to provide a stable base.

Draw the pattern on the melon as shown.

Use a sharp knife to cut out the section to be used for the handle.
Use a decorating tool or knife to cut the fancy edges of the buggy.

Remove the top section of rind. Hollow the buggy and attach the handle with toothpicks.

Attach wheels made from orange slices and hubcaps made from strawberries.
Fill the buggy with desired fruit.

Chariot

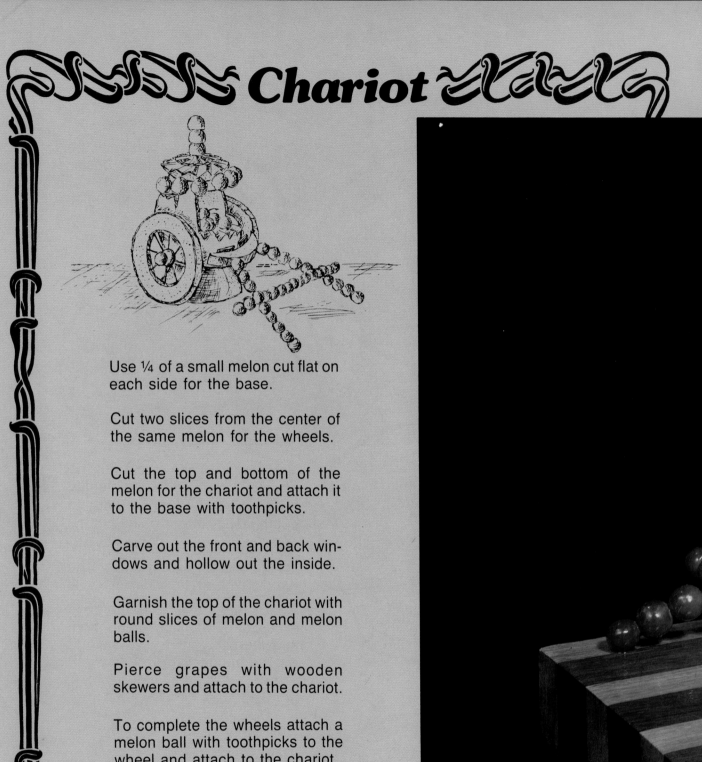

Use ¼ of a small melon cut flat on each side for the base.

Cut two slices from the center of the same melon for the wheels.

Cut the top and bottom of the melon for the chariot and attach it to the base with toothpicks.

Carve out the front and back windows and hollow out the inside.

Garnish the top of the chariot with round slices of melon and melon balls.

Pierce grapes with wooden skewers and attach to the chariot.

To complete the wheels attach a melon ball with toothpicks to the wheel and attach to the chariot.

Fill the chariot with fresh fruit and decorate the background with lemon leaves or ferns.

Cut a thin slice from the bottom of the melon to create a stable base. Cut off approximately 1/5 from the end of the watermelon and save this piece for the rear of the roadster to be attached later.

Trim the rind from the melon and carve the flesh into the body of the roadster as shown.

Hollow out the back section of the watermelon which will be the seating area of the roadster.

The rear of the roadster is made from the end 1/5 section that was first cut off.

Trim off the rind and carve the rear section as shown, then attach it to the body with toothpicks.

The wheels are made from slices of cataloupe.

Trim some of the flesh to form the wheels, insert toothpicks for spokes and melon balls for hub caps.

Attach the wheels to the body with toothpicks.

Carve the fenders and bumpers from curved sections of rind and attach with toothpicks.

The spare tire is made from a round slice of melon decorated with V-wedge cuts and attached to the body with toothpicks.

Carve the windshield from a curved section of rind and attach it to the body.

The front and rumble seat is made from pieces of melon carved and decorated with V-wedge cuts and attached to the body with toothpicks.

Carve the grill and hood ornament from sections of rind, decorate with V-wedge cuts and attach.

Reindeer and Sled

Using stencils made from the diagrams provided draw and then carve the end of a melon into the sections for the sled and reindeer.

Contour the flesh as shown. Attach the antlers and tails to the bodies with toothpicks and use cloves for eyes.

Mount the reindeer on melon slices decorated with twigs and baby's breath.

Connect the sled sections with toothpicks and fill with fruit.

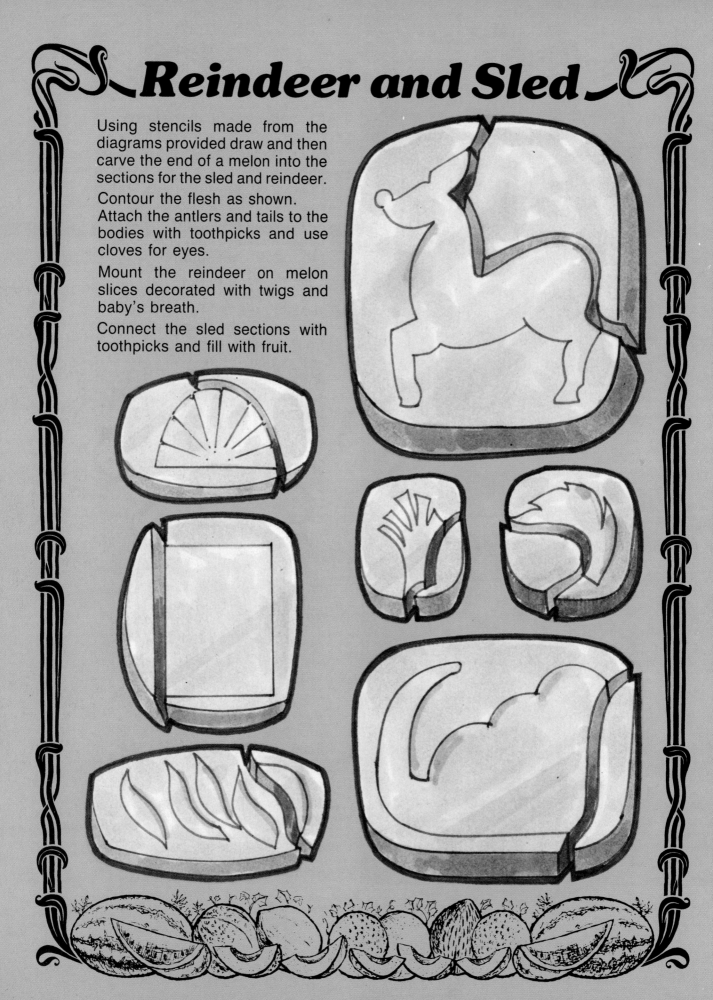

Melon Music

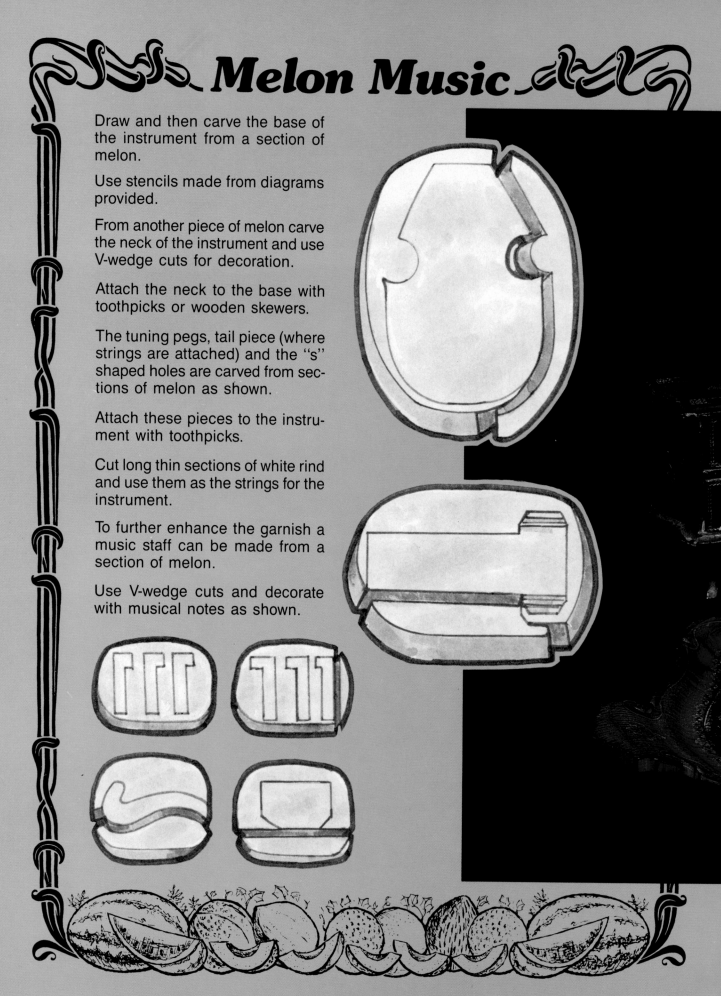

Draw and then carve the base of the instrument from a section of melon.

Use stencils made from diagrams provided.

From another piece of melon carve the neck of the instrument and use V-wedge cuts for decoration.

Attach the neck to the base with toothpicks or wooden skewers.

The tuning pegs, tail piece (where strings are attached) and the "s" shaped holes are carved from sections of melon as shown.

Attach these pieces to the instrument with toothpicks.

Cut long thin sections of white rind and use them as the strings for the instrument.

To further enhance the garnish a music staff can be made from a section of melon.

Use V-wedge cuts and decorate with musical notes as shown.

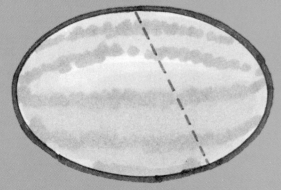

Cut the end of an oblong melon diagonally as shown.

Place the melon cut-side down and cut it lengthwise through the center.

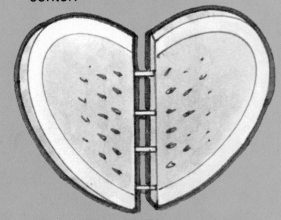

Attach these two sections together to form a heart.
Secure with toothpicks and wooden skewers.
Remove the flesh from the center and fill with fruit.

Bases

Bases can be made from any of the many melon varieties.

They are used to provide stability, height and dimension to melon sculptures.

The base should not be too large or overly detailed so that it becomes the focal point.

The base should compliment and not overshadow the principal object.

Bases can be carved into boulders, waves or other solid objects to fit the specific theme of the display.

An example is to place the seahorses on a base of waves.

Pictured here are several of the many types of bases that can be made.

You may want to try one without removing the outer rind or by carving into the rind with V-wedge cuts.

The V-wedge cut can be used to add a sculptured look and different varieties of melons can be combined to form an eye-pleasing arrangement when stacked on top of each other.

Ferns, lemon leaves and greens of any type add the finishing touch to the proper chosen base.

Arrangement Containers

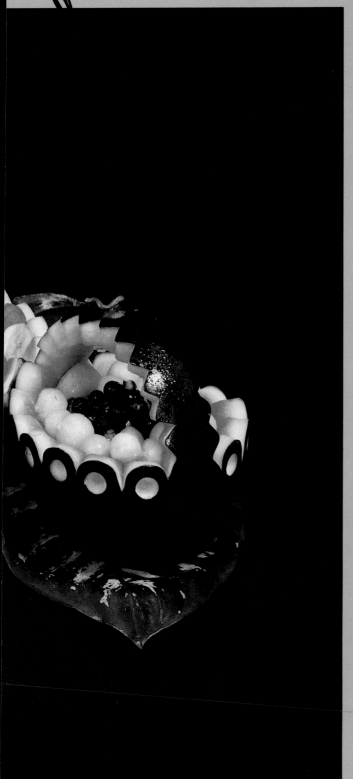

Arrangement containers can be made from any melon variety.

Draw or trace the outline of the desired pattern on the outside of the melon.

With a sharp knife or decorator tool follow the pattern you have traced and carefully cut away the unwanted rind.

Do not attempt to remove large areas of unwanted rind in one piece.

If the container you choose to make has a handle, it is most helpful to remove large pieces of unwanted rind by cutting into quarter sections.

Scoop out the basket area of the container with a melon ball tool.

Fill the container with melon balls, blueberries, strawberries or desired mixed fruit.

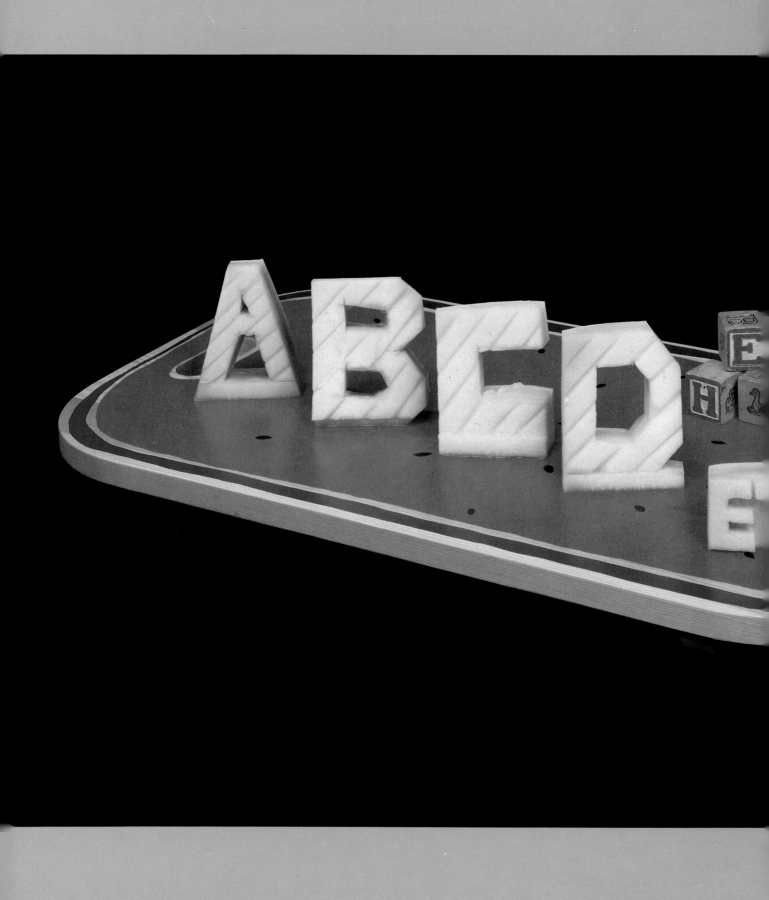

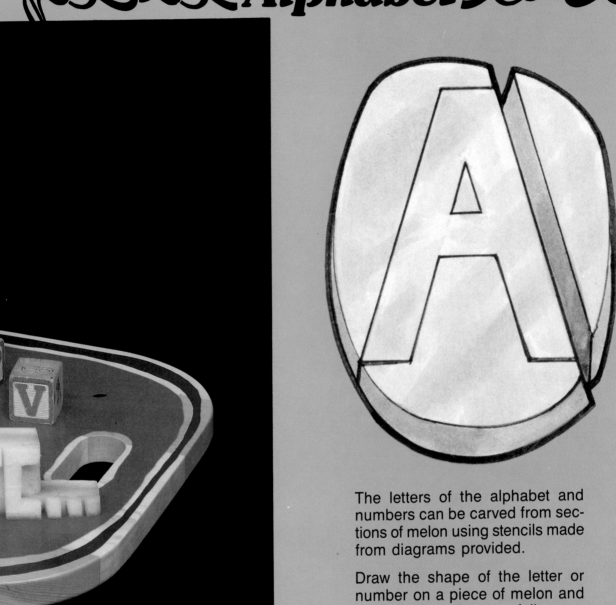

The letters of the alphabet and numbers can be carved from sections of melon using stencils made from diagrams provided.

Draw the shape of the letter or number on a piece of melon and use a sharp knife to carefully carve the contour.

Names, birthdays, holidays and anniversary messages can be spelled out using the carved letters and numbers.

Decorate the letters with V-wedge cuts and display as desired.

Flying Swan

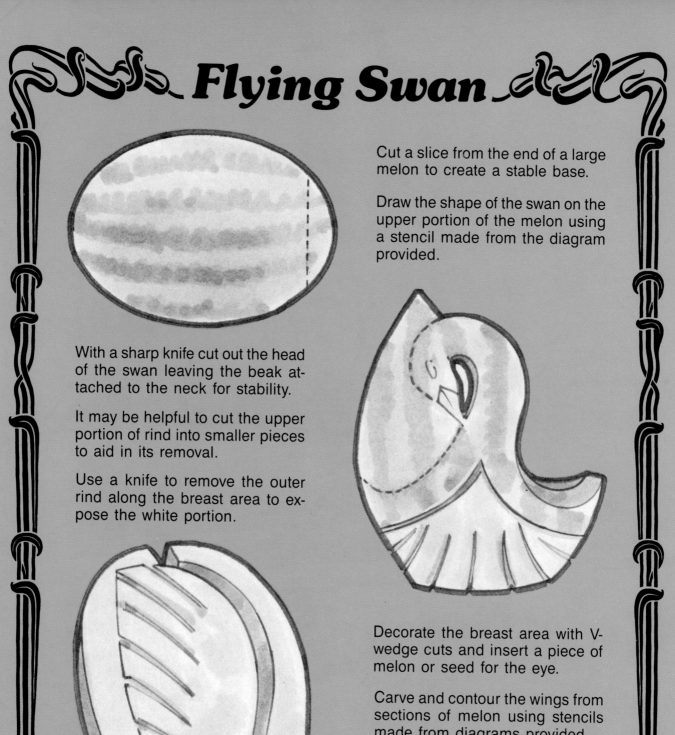

Cut a slice from the end of a large melon to create a stable base.

Draw the shape of the swan on the upper portion of the melon using a stencil made from the diagram provided.

With a sharp knife cut out the head of the swan leaving the beak attached to the neck for stability.

It may be helpful to cut the upper portion of rind into smaller pieces to aid in its removal.

Use a knife to remove the outer rind along the breast area to expose the white portion.

Decorate the breast area with V-wedge cuts and insert a piece of melon or seed for the eye.

Carve and contour the wings from sections of melon using stencils made from diagrams provided.

Use V-wedge cuts to form the feathers and attach the wings to the basket with wooden skewers.

Hollow the basket and fill with desired fruit.

Melon Varieties

1	HONEY DEW
2	ORANGE FLESH MELON
3	SHARLYN
4	CASABA
5	CHARLESTON GREY
6	JUBILEE
7	CRIMSON SWEET
8	SANTA CLAUS
9	PERSIAN
10	CRENSHAW
11	JUAN CANARY
12	CANTALOUPE